PricewaterhouseCoopers
Guide to the
2005 Tax Rules

PricewaterhouseCoopers

Guide to the 2005 Tax Rules

Includes the Latest 2005 Income Tax Numbers!

PricewaterhouseCoopers LLP

WILEY

John Wiley & Sons, Inc.

Published by John Wiley & Sons, Inc., Hoboken, New Jersey.

Published simultaneously in Canada.

For general information on our other products and services, or technical support, please contact our Customer Care Department within the United States at 800-762-2974, outside the United States at 317-572-3993 or fax 317-572-4002.

Wiley also publishes its books in a variety of electronic formats. Some content that appears in print may not be available in electronic books.

Library of Congress Cataloging-in-Publication Data:

PricewaterhouseCoopers guide to the 2005 tax rules /
PricewaterhouseCoopers.
     p. cm.
"Includes the Latest 2005 Income Tax Numbers!"
Includes index.
  ISBN 0-471-68615-8 (pbk.)
  1. Tax planning—United States. 2. Income tax—Law and legislation—United States. I. Title: Guide to the new tax rules.
KF6297.P75   2004
343.7305'2—dc22

                                  2003017974

Printed in the United States of America.
10 9 8 7 6 5 4 3 2 1

ACKNOWLEDGMENTS

A publication of this kind does not come together without the invaluable contributions of many. In particular, we would like to thank Paul Bracaglia, William Fleming, Richard Kohan, Christine Lamprecht, Paul Lanza, Peter Merrill, Daniel Noakes, Paul Schlather, Scott Torgan, Joe Walshe, and Karl Weger, for their important contributions.

This book is dedicated to the many partners and professionals of PricewaterhouseCoopers LLP who have spent a significant portion of their careers working with clients in developing strategies designed to help build, preserve, and maximize wealth.

MICHAEL B. KENNEDY
Partner, Human Resource Services, National Director of Personal Financial Services Practice

BERNARD S. KENT
Partner, Human Resource Services, Personal Financial Services Practice

CONTENTS

INTRODUCTION

To life's two proverbial certainties—death and taxes—we can safely add a third related one: tax *changes.* Year-in and year-out, the Internal Revenue Code presents a moving target. Congress, while keeping up a steady stream of complaints about the Tax Code's complexity and impenetrability, just can't seem to leave it alone. Whether there's a major overhaul or relatively minor tinkering, there is always something new to worry about or to profit from. Sometimes fairness or simplification is the goal; other times it's a break just for a small group of taxpayers; occasionally it's across-the-board relief.

In the past several years, Congress has made a great number of changes that phase-in over several years, take effect at different times or expire at set dates. Layered on this complexity are more than two dozen rules that are adjusted annually for inflation. These varying dates and inflation adjustments make using the new rules and planning for tomorrow extremely confusing and complex. And, as we go to press, Congress is poised to make additional changes that you want to watch out for.

How can you keep up with all the changes and know which of them can help you save money and plan for your future? This book gives you the tools you need to begin to sort things out and put them straight. It identifies the major areas of the tax law that have been or will be changed, including individual income tax rate reductions, reduced capital gains and dividends tax rates, an increased child credit, marriage penalty relief, and estate tax relief. It also shows how to use liberalized tax breaks to pay for education costs and how to maximize the expanded tax breaks for company-sponsored retirement plans and IRAs.

This book spells out the most important features of all these changes as well as the impact of important business tax breaks. It clearly explains the opportunities they offer for new tax-saving advantages and strategies now and in the coming years.

Who We Are

We are personal financial services professionals in the Human Resource Services practice at PricewaterhouseCoopers, one of the leading worldwide organizations of tax advisors, accountants, and auditors. The firm operates in 139 countries and territories, advising large and small businesses, individuals, governments, and not-for-profit organizations. Our strategy is built on our commitment to develop our own people to be creative and effective team players devoted to producing outstanding quality service. We bring the ability to take fresh perspectives, to think differently, and to develop and implement new and value-adding solutions. Over 350 personal financial services professionals in the United States provide high net worth individuals with comprehensive financial planning services, including estate and gift tax planning, income tax consulting and preparation, compensation and stock option planning, investment advisory services, retirement planning, and charitable giving strategies.

How to Use This Book

Chapter by chapter, we clarify the vital sections of new tax rules, with concrete examples that tell taxpayers what they need to know to build a solid base for planning and then to begin to map their own dollar-saving strategies. However, oversimplification is dangerous. We strongly recommend that taxpayers understand at least the basic provisions of the law before planning—that is why we wrote this book.

Here's what lies ahead:

- Chapter 1 spells out the key elements of the tax changes at work today, explaining briefly what each major provision and change does, how it works, and its timing.

- The laws' impact on investments and stock options is the subject of Chapter 2. There are major changes that will affect most investment plans.

- Retirement planning should be part of each taxpayer's strategy from the time he or she begins work. Chapter 3 discusses how to make planning for retirement a reality, and what changes in planning the new laws will entail.

- The tax advantages of home ownership have been accepted wisdom for decades. But Chapter 4 explores the subtle differences the new laws will make when it comes to owning a home.

- The escalating costs of higher education can make paying tuition and other expenses difficult. Fortunately, the tax law provides incentives for both saving for education in the future as well as paying for education now. Chapter 5 covers how to maximize tax-law opportunities to save and pay for education.

- Paying for medical expenses has become more challenging as health care costs continue to rise. Tax law changes, explained in Chapter 6, provide some important options for paying health care costs on a tax-advantaged basis.

- How can you structure your estate for a time when the "death tax" is gradually phasing out, only to reappear after 2010? Chapter 7 offers estate planning ideas.

- Chapter 8 sums up important strategies for year-end tax planning in a quick planning guide.

- When preparing your taxes, moving deductions to the previous tax year can save significant dollars. Chapter 9 describes those deductions that may be best to accelerate.

- Chapter 10 applies the same year-end tax saving principles to deferring income from one year to the next, when it may be taxed less under scheduled changes.

- Chapter 11 describes the alternative minimum tax (AMT), discusses who may be subject to the tax, and explains the tax planning implications.

- Year-end planning for business owners incorporates all of the personal strategies previously discussed, but doesn't end there. There are many additional considerations that can generate tax savings for business owners and for their companies that can be found in Chapter 12.

- Chapter 13 explains basic tax concepts as they have evolved in the Tax Code and puts the recent changes into context.

Interspersed through each chapter are a number of special features. Most of these are *Observations*—brief, clear explanations of specific features of the new law and how they will be applied. There are also occasional passages labeled *Caution,* warning of a possible blunder taxpayers might make based on a misinterpretation of the law. *Legislative alerts* are highlighted to warn you of possible changes to come. Congress may enact these changes after this book has been completed. In addition, most chapters contain an *Idea Checklist,* offering readers a quick summary of concepts to be used for taking advantage of today's favorable tax rules.

Congress Passes American Jobs Creation Act

As we went to press, Congress passed the American Jobs Creation Act of 2004 (referred to as "the Act" on this page). This significant tax legislation principally affects business taxpayers. There are a few items in the Act which are of interest to individual taxpayers and make some slight changes to this book.

The most important provision affecting individuals is a new election to deduct state and local general sales tax. The Act allows taxpayers who itemize their deductions to deduct state and local sales and use taxes instead of deducting state and local income taxes. States that do not impose an individual income tax generally have higher sales tax rates. Sales taxes were deductible prior to 1987. The Act attempts to eliminate the disparity in deductibility of the different methods of state financing.

Individuals who elect to deduct their sales tax have two choices. One alternative is to deduct the actual sales and use tax for the year. Taxpayers may find it difficult to calculate their actual sales tax for 2004 since there was no reason to accumulate this data for tax purposes until the Act was passed. The other choice is to deduct an amount determined from IRS tables which will be based on income, number of dependents, and other factors. The sales tax on motor vehicles and boats can be added to the IRS table amounts.

Taxpayers who pay state income taxes may be better off taking the deduction for sales tax if they have significant purchases subject to sales and use tax. This is particularly true if they are building a house and the sales tax on the cost of materials is separately stated by the contractor. Taxpayers who pay alternative minimum tax will not benefit from the sales and use tax deduction, and this deduction will increase the number of taxpayers who are affected by the alternative minimum tax.

(continued)

Continued

Taxpayers who may benefit from the sales tax deduction should carefully plan their large purchases at year end and whether to pay fourth quarter state and local income tax estimated payments in December or January.

On page 236, we mention that the entire purchase price of vehicles weighing over 6,000 pounds can be deducted in the year of acquisition if used 100 percent for business purposes. The ability to write off the full cost of a sports utility vehicle that is used for business transportation was viewed as an unintended benefit by many in Congress. The Act reduces the amount of first year depreciation that can be claimed on the purchase of a sports utility vehicle that is used in a trade or business to $25,000, effective for property placed in service after the date of enactment.

On page 199, we caution that the IRS is looking closely at charitable contributions of autos. The Act limits the deduction for charitable contributions of vehicles after 2004 to the amount received by the charity upon sale, unless the charity has made significant use of the vehicle in its charitable activity. The new rules apply to motor vehicles, boats, and airplanes.

Let's Get Started

It is human, and normal, to be intimidated by the subject of taxes. For most of us, our dealings with the Internal Revenue Service won't end with a royal tap on the shoulder, but we can benefit greatly if we take the initiative and make the effort to overcome such fears. When it comes to taxes, forewarned is forearmed. An investment of time and effort in forming a strategy for the coming years will pay off, year after year.

Tax Rate Reduction and Other Changes

Chapter 1

THE NEW AND IMPROVED TAX CLIMATE

The old saying that something is "as changeable as the weather" could just as easily be "as changeable as the Tax Code." Hardly a year goes by without at least some tinkering by Congress. But every couple of decades—most recently in the early 1960s and again in the early 1980s—there are changes to the Tax Code that require people fundamentally rethink all of their tax planning strategies. Their old approaches no longer work. Once again major tax changes in this millennium necessitate that people reconsider their tax situations and, perhaps, their personal lives. Reductions in tax rates on both ordinary income as well as capital gains and dividends have been dramatic. Marriage penalty relief reduces the tax bite on working couples. Increased savings opportunities now exist for retirement plans and for education. There are new ways to pay medical costs on a tax-advantaged basis. Federal estate taxes are declining for the moment. And numerous tax breaks have been created for special categories of individuals.

To better understand how all the changes fit together, here is an overview of rate reductions and other new rules. These changes and the planning opportunities they present will be fleshed out in greater detail throughout the book.

- **Rate reductions, tax credits, and deductions.** Before rate reduction began in 2001, the top rate on individuals was 39.6 percent; today it is only 35 percent. The bottom rate was 15 percent; today it is 10 percent. The child credit was added, then increased to $1,000. The credit for childcare expenses has been increased. Limits on personal exemptions and itemized deductions for high-income taxpayers will be phased out by 2010. There is limited relief from the alternative minimum tax (AMT). Married people who pay more tax than they would as singles have some relief from the hated marriage penalty.

- **Investment changes.** The tax rates on dividends and long-term capital gains have been cut substantially. The capital gains tax rates for noncorporate taxpayers, which previously were 10 percent or 20 percent, are now 15 percent (5 percent for those in the two lowest income tax brackets). These new lower rates apply for both regular tax and alternative minimum tax purposes.

- **Education reforms.** Coverdell Education Savings Accounts, which replaced education IRAs, were overhauled to quadruple the contribution limit. Section 529 plans, which previously were only state-sponsored programs to save for tuition and expenses at colleges and universities, have been expanded to include plans of private institutions. Deductibility of interest on student loans has also been expanded, and there now is a deduction of up to $4,000 in college tuition.

- **Retirement plan changes.** Incentives for retirement savings have been vastly improved for employees and self-employed individuals. Contribution limits have been raised for IRAs, with additional contribution amounts for those age 50 and older. And there is a special tax credit to help low-income taxpayers save for retirement.

- **Estate tax changes.** Reforms of the so-called *death tax* have created considerable estate planning complexities for the wealthiest 2 percent of taxpayers—those who may owe estate taxes on their accumulated wealth when they die. The amount that can be passed at death free of federal estate tax has grown so that many may think that they no longer need be concerned with estate tax planning. But planning is still vital. First, federal estate tax cuts (culminating in no estate tax in 2010) are temporary; after 2010, old estate tax rules are poised to take hold again. And state tax rules may now apply to estates that might otherwise have escaped this level of taxation. No doubt, there will be more changes ahead. Based on the November 2004 election, you can rest assured, the tax climate won't remain static. We next discuss these and other changes, and what they portend for individual taxpayers, in more detail.

Rate Reductions, Tax Credits, and Deductions

Tax rates used to be as high as 90 percent. But high tax rates are a thing of the past. Tax rates have come down over the years and recent reductions now provide a top tax rate of 35 percent. Because our tax system uses graduated tax rates, higher-income taxpayers also benefit from rate reductions in the lower tax brackets.

10 Percent Income Tax Bracket

There is now a 10 percent tax bracket, which benefits all taxpayers. For 2005 (after taking adjustment for inflation into account), the 10 percent bracket applies to:

- The first $7,300 of taxable income for single individuals.
- The first $10,450 of taxable income for heads of households.
- The first $14,600 of taxable income for married couples filing joint returns.

Legislative Alert

Congress recently passed an extension of the 10 percent tax bracket, indexed for inflation, through 2010.

Reduction in 28 Percent and Higher Tax Rates

The top four tax brackets, which had been 28 percent, 31 percent, 36 percent, and 39.6 percent, have been reduced to 25 percent, 28 percent, 33 percent, and 35 percent, respectively.

2003 Tax Rates (%)	2004 Tax Rates (%)
27	25
30	28
35	33
38.6	35

These rates apply through 2010, after which they are scheduled to increase back to 28 percent, 31 percent, 36 percent, and 39.6 percent.

Caution

The reduction in the regular income tax rates increases the likelihood that taxpayers will be subject to the alternative minimum tax (AMT). The reason: As the regular tax declines through lower tax rates and new deductions, it is more likely that AMT will exceed it, creating AMT liability. To help offset this problem, at least for now, the AMT exemption amount has been increased. Taxpayers more susceptible to the AMT include those with significant capital gains and dividend income, and those who live in states with high state income tax rates. Taxpayers who are in the 28 percent, 33 percent, or 35 percent marginal tax bracket and receive dividend income may find themselves subject to AMT due to the disparity in the rates between AMT and regular tax (see Chapter 2 for details).

Observation

Congress's Joint Committee on Taxation estimates that 2.4 million taxpayers will be subject to the AMT in 2003; 2.9 million in 2004. The National Taxpayer Advocate reported to Congress that the number of taxpayers affected by the AMT could hit 12.5 million in 2005 and 30 million by 2010 if something isn't done. The general consensus is that Washington will have to come up with a more permanent solution to the AMT problem or suffer the political consequences. But the increasing budget deficits will make finding a solution elusive.

Caution

The lower tax rates generally increase the after-tax cost of making charitable contributions.

Observation

Generally, the reduction in marginal rates, particularly the creation of the 10 percent income tax bracket, enhances the tax advantage of moving ordinary income such as interest over to children age 14 and older. People in the top income bracket, for example, can save 25 percent in taxes by shifting up to $7,300 in income to a child. That is the difference between the 10 percent bracket and the top 35 percent bracket. As explained later in this chapter and in more detail in Chapter 2, shifting capital gains and dividends to low-bracket children also can be advantageous. (Be careful about this, however, because the unearned income of children under age 14 in excess of $1,600 is taxed under the so-called *kiddie tax* rules at the parents' marginal tax rate.)

Observation

The reduction in marginal rates would appear to make tax-exempt investments, such as municipal bonds, relatively less attractive. However, the comparative yields on municipal bonds are generally attractive for high-bracket taxpayers even with the lower marginal tax rates.

Observation

The reduction in marginal rates also benefits owners of pass-through entities, such as partnerships, limited liability companies, and S corporations, each of which subjects its owner to only one level of individual taxation.

Upper-Income Individuals Won't Lose Deductions

After 2005, the overall limitation on itemized deductions, which now reduces the value of certain itemized deductions claimed by higher income individuals, will be phased out. In effect, higher income individuals will have an even greater rate reduction.

In 2005, itemized deductions—except medical expenses; casualty, theft, or gambling losses; and investment interest expense—are reduced by 3 percent of the individual's adjusted gross income (AGI) above $145,950 for unmarried people as well as married couples filing joint returns ($72,975 for married individuals filing separately). Although these amounts are adjusted annually for inflation, this rule can cause you to lose as much as 80 percent of deductions in this category.

Personal Exemptions Won't Be Lost

The reduction of personal exemptions that is now imposed on higher income taxpayers is phased out. Beginning after 2005, those affected will receive what is, in effect, an additional tax rate reduction.

Currently, deductions for personal exemptions ($3,100 each in 2004) are reduced or eliminated at higher income levels. For 2004, the deduction must be reduced by 2 percent for each $2,500 ($1,250 for married people filing separately) or a portion of $2,500 that the taxpayer's AGI exceeds $214,050 for joint returns; $107,025 for married couples filing separately; $178,350 for heads of households; and $142,700 for single individuals. For 2004, personal exemptions are completely phased out at $336,550 on joint returns; $168,275 for married individuals filing separate returns; $300,850 for heads of household; and $265,200 for single individuals (see Chapter 13 for 2005 figures).

The personal exemption phase-out will be reduced by one-third for 2006 and 2007; two-thirds for 2008 and 2009; and eliminated altogether after that.

Marriage Penalty Relief

Working couples may experience a marriage penalty. This occurs when a husband and wife each work and earn about the same money. They pay more in tax together than they would pay if they were single. Fortunately, there has been some relief created:

- **Standard deduction increase.** The basic standard deduction for married couples is now twice the standard deduction for single filers.

- **Expansion of the 15 percent bracket.** The 15 percent income tax bracket for married couples filing joint returns is now twice the size of the 15 percent bracket for single filers.

Legislative Alert

Congress recently passed a law extending the standard deduction increase (twice the standard deduction for single filers) as well as the expanded 15 percent income tax bracket for married couples filing jointly. These provisions now expire after 2010.

Observation

Married couples who itemize their deductions do not benefit from this change if their itemized deductions already exceed twice the standard deduction amount for single filers.

Observation

Unlike the change in the standard deduction, which only benefits people who do not itemize, the expansion of the 15 percent tax bracket helps all married couples with taxable income in this or higher brackets (as long as they are not subject to the AMT) because more of their income is taxed at a lower rate.

The Bottom Line

Combining the tax reductions discussed thus far, including the reduced tax rates on capital gains and dividend income, how much of tax reduction can an individual expect year by year? To answer that, let's look at a married couple who files jointly, has two dependent children, $500,000 of income ($430,000 of wages and interest, $50,000 of long-term capital gain, and $20,000 of qualified dividend income), and $50,000 of itemized deductions. Here's how much they save in 2004 (compared with the old tax rules):

Year	Tax ($)	Savings over Prior Law ($)
2001–Prior law	144,578	0
2004–Reduction in marginal, capital gain, and dividend tax rates, and increase in the size of the lower tax brackets	118,143	26,435

In 2010, they can save an additional $5,200 from the elimination of the phase-out of itemized deductions and personal exemptions at higher income levels. But after 2008, their tax would be higher because the tax rate on capital gains would rise from 15 percent to 20 percent, and the tax on their dividends would increase from 15 percent to 35 percent.

Child Tax Credit

A taxpayer with dependent children younger than age 17 may be entitled to a child tax credit of $1,000 per child. However, the credit begins to phase out once the modified adjusted gross income (AGI with some adjustments that do not affect most taxpayers) reaches $110,000 on a joint return ($75,000 for single individuals or heads of households and $55,000 for married couples filing separately). In general, the child tax credit is nonrefundable, which means that a refund is not issued if its total exceeds the tax owed. However, the credit may be refundable to some taxpayers, providing them money from the government in excess of the amount of taxes they paid.

Legislative Alert
Congress has recently extended the $1,000 child tax credit through 2010.

Currently, the amount of the refundable credit is 10 percent of taxable earned income in excess of $10,750 in 2004. The percentage will increase to 15 percent starting in 2005. If taxable income is not over $10,750, a refundable tax credit can still be claimed by a family with three or more children, to the extent that Social Security taxes exceed the earned income credit. Also, the child credit can be used to offset the AMT.

Adoption Credit

The tax law encourages the adoption of children. In 2004, a credit of up to $10,390 may be claimed for adopting a child. For those who adopt a child with special needs, the credit can be claimed without regard to expenses paid in the adoption. Alternatively, employees can receive income-tax-free a maximum of $10,390 for qualified adoption expenses paid by their employers. Both the credit and exclusion phased out at modified AGI levels between $155,860 and $195,860 in 2004.

Reminder
Unlike some other personal tax credits, the adoption credit can be claimed against the AMT.

Dependent Care Credit

A credit is allowed for certain dependent care expenses incurred on behalf of a child under age 13, or older dependents incapable of caring for themselves to enable parents to work. The amount of expenses eligible for credit under dependent care in 2004 is $3,000 ($6,000 for two or more qualifying children or dependents).

The maximum credit rate for those with adjusted gross income of $15,000 or less is 35 percent. It is reduced by one percentage point for each additional $2,000 of AGI, until it is reduced to 20 percent for those with AGI over $43,000. For example, an individual with two qualifying children and an AGI of $29,000 is entitled to a maximum credit of $1,680 (28 percent of $6,000). Taxpayers with two or more qualifying children or dependents and income over $43,000 are entitled to a maximum credit of $1,200 (20 percent of $6,000).

Alternative Minimum Tax

The alternative minimum tax (AMT) was intended to ensure that high-income taxpayers who benefit from various deductions, credits, and exemptions pay at least a minimum amount of tax. The AMT is calculated by reducing or eliminating the tax benefits that have been claimed for regular income tax purposes. Next, the exemption amount is subtracted, and the AMT tax rates (26 percent up to $175,000 and 28 percent above that amount) are applied to the balance. The taxpayer then compares the result with his or her regular tax and pays the higher amount. The AMT exemption is available for taxpayers with relatively modest incomes. For 2004 and 2005, the exemption amount is $58,000 for married couples filing jointly and $40,250 for single taxpayers.

The exemption phases out for married taxpayers with AMT between $150,000 and $382,000. For single taxpayers the phase out is between $112,500 and $273,500. The AMT tax rates remain at 26 percent for the first $175,000 of AMT income ($87,500 for married individuals filing separately) after the exemption, and 28 percent for the balance.

Example

The following example illustrates how taxpayers with only regular income (not capital gains or dividends) will pay more AMT under the new tax law merely because the regular tax rates are reduced: See Chapter 2 for the impact of capital gains and dividend income on AMT liability.

Observation

Although the AMT exemption has been increased slightly, tax-payers subject to the AMT may not realize the reductions in the regular income tax rates. Furthermore, the regular income tax rate reductions themselves will increase many people's exposure to the AMT.

Regular Taxable Income (No Dividends or Capital Gains)	$175,000	$325,000	$500,000
Old law regular tax due	42,781.50	95,751.30	163,301.30
New law regular tax due	38,958.00	88,393.00	149,643.00
State income taxes	14,000	20,000	40,000
Other disallowed deductions	25,000	25,000	25,000
AMTI	214,000	370,000	565,000
AMT exemption allowed	42,000	3,000	0
Old tentative minimum tax	47,180	100,100	154,700
New tentative minimum tax	44,720	99,260	154,700
Old alternative minimum tax	4,398.50	4,348.70	0
New alternative minimum tax	5,762.00	10,867.00	5,057.00

Legislative Alert

Congress has recently extended the current $58,000 AMT exemption for married couples filing jointly ($40,250 for single taxpayers) through 2005.

Investment Changes

The top rate on most capital gains is now 15 percent. This rate also applies to qualified dividends. Here are the details.

Long-Term Capital Gains

For sales and exchanges of capital assets and for installment-sale payments received after May 5, 2003, the rates are:

- 15 percent for those in regular tax brackets above 15 percent
- 5 percent (zero, in 2008) for those in the 10 or 15 percent rate brackets

The rates apply to capital assets held for more than one year. They apply both for regular tax and AMT purposes. A 28 percent rate on collectibles and the taxable portion of gain on qualified small business stock, and the 25 percent rate that applies to depreciation recapture on the sale of buildings for taxpayers in tax brackets above these rates.

After 2008, the tax rates on long-term capital gains revert to the previous 20 percent rate (10 percent for those in the two lowest tax brackets). Also the special capital gains rate of 18 percent (8 percent for those in the two lowest tax brackets) for assets held more than five years again applies.

Reduced Dividend Rates

Qualified dividends received by individuals are taxed at the same rate as the tax on capital gains, or 15 percent (5 percent for individuals below the 25 percent tax bracket). The reduced rates on dividends apply through December 31, 2008.

Caution

To qualify for the special rate on dividends, stock must be held for more than 60 days during the 121-day period that begins 60 days before the ex-dividend date in order for a dividend to qualify for the preferential rates. For dividends paid on preferred stock that represent payments of dividend arrearages in excess of one year, however, the required holding period is 90 days during the 181-day period that begins 90 days before the ex-dividend date. The holding period is extended by any days on which the shareowner has diminished the risk of loss through options or other means.

Not all dividends qualify. Dividends paid by mutual savings banks, exempt organizations, and farmers' co-ops don't qualify for the reduced rates. Nor do dividends that the shareholder is obliged to pay to someone else, such as in connection with a short sale. Nor do dividends qualify that the shareholder elects to treat as investment income against which investment interest may be deducted. If a shareholder receives an extraordinary dividend that qualifies for the capital gains tax rates, any loss on the dividend-paying stock is a long-term capital loss to the extent of the extraordinary dividend.

Dividends from Pass-Through Entities

Qualified dividend income passed through from partnerships and bank common trust funds qualifies for the preferential capital gains rates. Qualified dividends passed through from mutual funds and REITs also generally qualify for the capital gain rates. However, certain distributions that generally are called dividends but really are not—such as life insurance policy dividends and money market fund dividends—do not qualify.

Observation

The current capital gains and dividend rates give investors a unique opportunity to reposition their portfolios and seek an allocation of investment assets that is better diversified and more consistent with their risk tolerance. Investors can sell their appreciated assets at a low tax rate of 15 percent and then reinvest the proceeds in a diversified portfolio of securities that can earn a higher rate of return for the level of risk assumed. Preferred stock with a high dividend yield and other income stocks can be more effectively combined with a portfolio of growth and value stocks to produce a more predictable after-tax rate of return now that dividends and capital gains are taxed at the same rate.

Education Reforms

Congress has recognized that the high cost of education is a problem for most taxpayers. To alleviate some of the burden, there are various tax incentives that make saving and paying for college easier.

Caution

Some of the education reforms created in recent years are scheduled to lapse after 2010, or sooner, unless Congress intervenes.

Coverdell Education Savings Accounts

The contribution to a Coverdell Education Savings Account (previously called an education IRA) cannot exceed a total of $2,000 from all donors. The $2,000 limit phases out for individuals with an

AGI over $95,000 and for married couples filing jointly with an AGI over $190,000.

Distributions from these accounts are tax-free up to the amount of the beneficiary's qualified education expenses in the year of distribution. The earnings portion of distributions that exceed those expenses in any given year is taxable and subject to a 10 percent penalty.

Qualified education expense includes the cost of kindergarten, elementary, and secondary school expenses (public, private, or religious), and certain after-school programs. Computer equipment, software, and Internet access also are included in this category. These qualified education expenses are in addition to the postsecondary education expenses permitted for Section 529 Qualified Tuition Plans (see Chapter 5).

A HOPE Scholarship credit, Lifetime Learning credit or tuition deduction may be claimed in the same year that a tax-free distribution is taken from a Coverdell Education Savings Account, as long as the same expenses aren't used to claim both the exclusion and a credit or deduction.

Contributions may be made to both a Coverdell Education Savings Account and to a qualified tuition program in the same year for the same beneficiary. In the past, such contributions could trigger an excise tax.

Observation

Parents should consider whether Coverdell Education Savings Accounts or Section 529 programs would affect their child's chances of receiving financial aid for college (see Chapter 5).

Section 529 Qualified Tuition Programs

College savings plans (known as Section 529 plans after the section of the Internal Revenue Code authorizing them) allow tuition credits to be purchased or contributions to be made to college savings accounts on behalf of a designated beneficiary. Private colleges and universities may establish prepaid tuition (but not savings) plans.

Distributions from these plans to pay qualified education costs are not taxable. Contributors are taxed on any refund from the program that exceeds the contributions made for a beneficiary.

Rollovers may be made from one plan to another once every 12 months without tax consequences, even if the beneficiary stays the same. The prior rule that allowed transfers between qualified accounts for different beneficiaries in the same family was expanded to include transfers that benefit a first cousin of the original beneficiary.

Observation

This modification enables grandparents to switch tuition-plan beneficiaries among their grandchildren.

The HOPE Scholarship credit, Lifetime Learning credit, and tuition deduction may be claimed in the same year that a distribution is taken from a qualified tuition plan, but the credit, deduction, and exclusion can't result from the same expenses.

Employer Education Assistance

An employer can pay up to $5,250 per year of educational expenses on behalf of an employee under an education-assistance plan. The benefit is tax free to the employee and exempt from payroll taxes. This benefit applies to both undergraduate and graduate-level courses, whether or not the courses are job-related.

Observation

Even without this specific tax break, reimbursements by employers for job-related courses, which are those that maintain or improve a skill currently used in the recipient's trade or business or are required to continue his or her employment, are tax free. This does not include courses that lead to a new profession.

Student Loan Interest Deduction

Taxpayers can deduct up to $2,500 annually for interest paid on qualified education loans. The maximum deduction is phased out for single taxpayers with AGI between $50,000 and $65,000, and for married taxpayers filing jointly with AGI between $105,000 and $135,000. The AGI limit will be adjusted for inflation. This interest deduction is available even to those who do not itemize deductions on their returns.

Deduction for Qualified Higher Education Expenses

In 2004 and 2005, a deduction can be claimed for qualified higher education expenses, by both itemizers and nonitemizers. The maximum deduction is $4,000 for those with an AGI of $65,000 ($130,000 for married couples filing jointly) or less. A deduction of $2,000 is available for those with AGI of more than $65,000, but not more than $80,000 (between $130,000 and $160,000 for married couples filing jointly). The deduction cannot be claimed in the same year as a HOPE Scholarship credit or a Lifetime Learning credit is claimed for the same student. Finally, taxpayers cannot deduct expenses taken into account when determining the amount of a Coverdell Education Savings Account or a tax-free qualified tuition plan distribution (see Table 1.1).

Table 1.1 *Highlights of Major Education Changes*		
Highlights	**Old Law**	**New Law**
Coverdell Education Savings Accounts contribution limit	$500	$2,000
AGI phase-out (single)	$95,000	$95,000
AGI phase-out (joint)	$150,000	$190,000
Qualified expenses	Higher education only	Elementary, secondary, and higher education
Section 529 plans		
Earnings used for education	Taxable	Tax-free
Employer Assistance Programs		
Eligible coursework	Postgraduate courses only	Undergraduate and postgraduate courses
Student loan interest deduction		
Interest payments eligible for	First 60 months payments	No limit
AGI phase-out range (single)	$40,000–$55,000	$50,000–$65,000
AGI phase-out range (joint)	$60,000–$75,000	$100,000–$130,000

Retirement Plan Changes

Employees and self-employed individuals have a greater opportunity to save for retirement today under current tax rules. The dollar limits on contributions have been increased and will continue to rise in the future. For example, the limit on contributions to a profit-sharing plan in 2005 is the lower of 100 percent of compensation or $42,000.

Observation

The 100 percent of compensation test (which had been 25 under old law) gives those individuals whose working histories are interrupted a chance to accumulate more retirement savings. While the increased limit applies to all plan participants, it is expected that second income spouses will be able to make the most use of it.

Caution

This change applies to the allocation limitation, not the deduction limitation.

Increase in Benefit Limit

The maximum annual benefit that a defined benefit pension plan can fund in 2005 is $170,000. The limit is reduced for benefits beginning before age 62 and increased for benefit payments commencing after age 65. This limit is adjusted annually for inflation.

Vesting of Employer Contributions

The tax law now requires more rapid vesting of employer-matching contributions to a qualified plan or 403(b) annuity. Employees' rights in these contributions become nonforfeitable either 100 percent after three years or 20 percent per year, beginning with the second year of service and increasing to 100 percent after six years of service. This vesting schedule applies only to employees who have some service after the 2000 plan year. These rules will also apply to collectively bargained plans in future years.

> **Caution**
>
> The new, more liberal vesting requirements do not apply to nonmatching employer contributions. Individuals' own plan contributions remain 100 percent vested at all times.

Increased Compensation Limit

The amount of compensation that can be taken into account for retirement plan purposes in 2005 is $210,000. The limit is adjusted annually for inflation in multiples of $5,000.

Increased 401(k) and SIMPLE Plan Deferrals

The annual elective deferral limit for 401(k) plans in 2004 is $13,000. It will increase in $1,000 increments until it reaches $15,000 in 2006. The same limits apply to 403(b) annuities and 457 deferred compensation arrangements.

The annual elective deferral limit for savings incentive match plans for employees (SIMPLE) plans that allow deferrals is $9,000 in 2004 and $10,000 in 2005.

All of these deferral limits will be indexed annually in $500 increments after the increases are fully phased in:

	Maximum Deferral Amount*	
	If Age Is Less Than 50 ($)	
Year	**401(k)**	**SIMPLE**
2004	13,000	9,000
2005	14,000	10,000
2006 and later	15,000 as indexed	10,000 as indexed

*Cannot exceed 100 percent of compensation.

> **Caution**
>
> A highly compensated employee (HCE) may not be allowed to take full advantage of the increased deferral limits after the 401(k) nondiscrimination tests are applied.

Catch-Up 401(k) and SIMPLE Plan Deferrals

Taxpayers can elect to make additional pre-tax deferrals if they are 50 years of age or older. These catch-up amounts are: $3,000 in 2004, $4,000 in 2005, and $5,000 in 2006 and thereafter. The additional catch-up amount allowed under a SIMPLE plan is $1,500 for 2004, increasing by $500 each year until it reaches $2,500 in 2006. The $5,000 and $2,500 amounts will be indexed for inflation after 2006.

The regular contribution limits and nondiscrimination rules do not apply to catch-up contributions provided the plan permits all eligible participants to make them. Employers are generally permitted, but not required, to match catch-up contributions.

	Maximum Deferral Amount* If at Least Age 50 ($) (Includes Catch-Up)	
Year	**401(k)**	**SIMPLE**
2004	16,000	10,500
2005	18,000	12,000
2006 and later	20,000 as indexed	12,500 as indexed

*Cannot exceed 100 percent of compensation.

Observation

Highly compensated employees and second-wage earners in families are more likely to have sufficient disposable income available to take advantage of the increases in the elective deferrals.

403(b) and 457 Plans

The increased limits for elective deferrals, including the catch-ups, apply in general to 403(b) annuities and to 457 deferred compensation arrangements maintained by a state government employer. However, a catch-up contribution cannot be made to a 457 arrangement in the three years prior to retirement. But special rules that apply only to 457 plans allow the annual deferral to be increased to twice the usual annual deferral limit. The rules that reduce the limits on contributions made to 457 plans by the amounts contributed to 403(b) and 401(k) plans have been repealed. This allows state government employees to increase retirement savings by making an elective deferral to a 457 plan and deferring the maximum amount to a 403(b) annuity or a 401(k) plan, as well.

Larger IRA Contributions

For nearly 20 years, the annual IRA contribution had been fixed at $2,000. Now it is $3,000. It will increase to $4,000 for 2005 through 2007, and to $5,000 for 2008. The new contribution limit will be indexed annually for inflation after 2008 in $500 increments. Those age 50 or older as of year-end can make a catch-up contribution.

Observation

An IRA owner doesn't have to wait to turn 50 before making catch-up contributions; the contributions can be made at any time during that fiftieth birthday year.

The maximum catch-up contributions are $500 through 2005 and $1,000 after 2005 as shown below:

	Increased IRA Contribution Limits	
Year	Regular IRA ($)	Catch-Up ($)
2004	3,000	500
2005	4,000	500
2006	4,000	1,000
2007	4,000	1,000
2008 and later	5,000	1,000

Observation

These increases will give taxpayers and their spouses more opportunities to save for retirement so they can rely less on employer retirement plans and Social Security. Over long periods of time, even relatively modest additional savings can accumulate significantly.

Observation

The income limits for deductible IRAs, eligibility for Roth IRAs, and converting regular IRAs into Roth IRAs remain unchanged. As a result, the only benefit that higher-income taxpayers, who are active participants in employer retirement plans (or whose spouses are), will realize from the IRA changes is the ability to make larger contributions to nondeductible regular IRAs.

IRA/Employer Plan Combination

Employees may now be able to save for retirement through payroll deductions. Employers can offer *Deemed IRAs,* which are accounts that meet all of the regular IRA requirements.

Roth IRA/Employer Plan Combination

Starting in 2006, employees may have a new way to save for retirement. Employers may allow them to make a *Qualified Roth Contribution*. Essentially this is a contribution to a 401(k) or 403(b) annuity as an after-tax contribution. While the earnings used to make the contribution will be taxable now, funds in the retirement plan will build up on a tax-free basis like a Roth IRA.

Even taxpayers whose incomes are too high to contribute to regular Roth IRAs can contribute to the new arrangements; the option will be available to all plan members. Thus, even high-income individuals can designate 401(k) deferrals as Roth IRA contributions if their plans are amended to permit it.

Observation

Taxpayers will need to balance current and future advantages and disadvantages of elective deferrals or Roth IRA contributions each year, taking into account the time until distribution and the potential marginal tax bracket at distribution.

Rollovers

It is now easier to move funds from one type of retirement plan to another. The law allows rollover contributions between regular retirement plans, such as 401(k) plans, tax-sheltered annuity plans (403(b) plans), and governmental retirement plans (Section 457 plans). After-tax contributions to employer plans can also be rolled over. Surviving spouse beneficiaries also have more choices on rollover plans.

Rollover Eligible Plans

Now 403(b) and 457 plans can accept rollovers from other plans. In the past, only IRAs and qualified plans could accept rollovers, and the latter could accept rollovers only from other qualified plans or from *conduit* IRAs (IRAs containing only rollovers from qualified plans); 403(b) plans could only accept rollovers from another 403(b) plan.

Observation

The rollover rules are especially valuable for those who accept jobs with the government or tax-exempt employers after working in the private sector.

Caution

Any grandfathered features (eligibility for 10-year averaging; capital gains for pre-1974 accruals; or tax deferral on unrealized appreciation from distributed employer securities) may be lost if a rollover is made.

Rollover of After-Tax Contributions

After-tax contributions from employer plans can be rolled over to IRAs along with the taxable portion of the account at retirement. It is now also possible to roll over after-tax contributions into a new employer plan, provided it is a direct trustee-to-trustee transfer. Rollovers of after-tax contributions must be accounted for separately. When they are distributed, special ordering rules apply for the after-tax account: Earnings are deemed to be distributed first and contributions last in such a transfer. Thus, before rolling over funds from a tax-qualified plan, you should determine your continuing eligibility for special tax rules.

Observation

Once an after-tax contribution is rolled over into an IRA, it cannot be rolled back into a qualified plan, 403(b) annuity or 457 plan. The downside is that after-tax contributions add a layer of complexity when distributions are taken from the account. The rules for recovering after-tax contributions from IRA distributions differ from those for pension distributions. For example, a participant in a qualified plan who receives a distribution of $500,000 (including $200,000 in after-tax contributions) can roll over $300,000, keep the $200,000 of after-tax contributions, and pay no tax. However, an IRA owner in the same situation would be taxed on 60 percent of the $200,000 that wasn't rolled into an IRA.

Spousal Rollovers

A surviving spouse can roll over an inherited IRA to his or her own employer-sponsored plan.

Caution

Although this change permits the surviving spouse to consolidate funds in a single location, rolling inherited IRA funds into a qualified plan may not be the best approach because the beneficiary payout features of qualified plans are usually not as flexible as IRA payout features. The surviving spouse can preserve greater flexibility for payouts to beneficiaries by using an IRA rollover.

Tax Credit for Plan Contributions

Through 2006, a nonrefundable tax credit is available to certain lower income individuals who contribute to qualified retirement plans (including IRAs and Roth IRAs). This credit is in addition to any other deduction available. The maximum annual contribution eligible for the credit is $2,000.

The credit rate phases down from 50 percent to 10 percent of the contribution based on the individual's AGI. It is only available to those with an AGI below the beginning of the IRA deduction phase-out and is totally phased out for those with an AGI above $50,000 for joint filers, $37,500 for head-of-household filers, and $25,000 for single filers. This credit is not available to students, taxpayers under age 18, or dependents.

Employer Provided Retirement Planning

Retirement planning services provided to employees and spouses can be a nontaxable fringe benefit. Highly compensated employees qualify for this exclusion only if services are available on substantially similar terms to all employees who normally receive information regarding the employer's qualified plan. Employers can probably limit the advice they offer to those who are at or near retirement age.

Observation

The exclusion is not available for other services associated with retirement planning, such as tax preparation, legal, accounting, or brokerage services.

Caution

Retirement planning involves complex income tax, investment, and logistic issues. Several professional groups participate in what has become a significant service industry, including accountants, attorneys, trust officers, financial planners, and brokers. This exclusion should provide employees with greater access to these services.

Required Minimum Distributions

Rules for required minimum distributions from IRAs and qualified retirement plans are now simpler than ever before. The new rules incorporate improved mortality experience.

Observation

The IRS revisions to the prior rules on distributions thoroughly simplify what was an overly complex process fraught with dangerous tax pitfalls.

Caution

A taxpayer who must take a minimum required distribution from an IRA should make sure it has been calculated using the latest rules. The revisions decrease by a significant degree the amount of required distributions for almost everyone (see Chapter 3 for details).

Plan Loans to Owner-Employees

S corporation owners, partners, and sole proprietors now may borrow from their retirement plans without being liable for the "prohibited transactions" excise tax. However, they must adhere to the rules that apply to plan loans made to other participants. Generally, this means the amounts that can be borrowed are limited to whichever is less: $50,000, or half the individual's account balance. Also, repayment with interest must be made at regular intervals over a term of no more than five years (longer for loans used to purchase a principal residence).

Small-Business Credit for Plan Start-Up Costs

To encourage small businesses to establish retirement plans for employees, there is a special tax credit. Costs to set up a new retirement plan are eligible for a nonrefundable income tax credit equal to 50 percent of the first $1,000 in administrative and retirement education expenses for each of the first three years of the plan. The 50 percent of qualifying expenses that is offset by the tax credit is not deductible; the other 50 percent (and all other expenses) is deductible as it is currently. The credit is available only to an employer that did not employ more than 100 employees who earned more than $5,000 in the preceding year. Also, at least one employee who is not highly compensated must be covered by the plan:

	2001 Tax Act ($)	Prior Law ($)
Deductible start-up cost	1,000	1,000
Plan education expense	1,000	1,000
Total qualifying expenses	2,000	2,000
Credit	500	0
Total deductible expenses	1,500	2,000
Tax savings* including credit	1,025	700
Net cost of plan	975	1,300

*Assuming a 35 percent tax bracket for individual owner.

Waiver of User Fees

Employer plans with 100 or fewer employees, and at least one participant who is not highly compensated pay no IRS fee to obtain an IRS determination letter request regarding the plan's qualified status during its first five years (or the end of any remedial amendment period that begins within those first five years).

"Top-Heavy" Rules

So-called *top-heavy retirement plans*—those in which key employees receive more than 60 percent of the contributions or benefits—

must provide certain minimum benefits or contribution levels to less-key employees and vest those benefits earlier than other plans are required to do. A *key employee* is one who, during the prior year, was an officer with compensation in excess of $130,000, a 5 percent owner, or a 1 percent owner with compensation in excess of $150,000.

Only distributions made in the year prior to the determination date (and in-service distributions during the previous five years) are taken into account when deciding whether the plan is top-heavy. Matching contributions may be taken into account in satisfying the minimum benefit requirements. A safe-harbor 401(k) plan is not a top-heavy plan, and matching or nonelective contributions provided under a safe-harbor plan may be taken into account in satisfying the minimum contribution requirements for top-heavy plans. Frozen defined benefit plans (or plans in which no key employee or former key employee benefits under the plan) are exempt from the minimum benefit requirements.

Increased Deduction Limits

Contribution limit increases, discussed earlier in this chapter, are not necessarily the same limit for figuring deductions.

- The deduction limit for stock bonus and profit-sharing plans is 25 percent of eligible compensation. Money purchase pension plans generally are treated like profit-sharing or stock bonus plans for purposes of the deduction limits.
- Employee elective deferrals are not subject to deduction limits and are not taken into account for purposes of applying the deduction limits to other types of contributions.
- For purposes of the deduction limits, the definition of *compensation* includes salary reduction amounts under a Section 125 cafeteria plan and 401(k) elective deferrals.

Observation

These changes eliminate the need to have a profit-sharing plan in tandem with a money purchase plan because they provide the maximum deduction of 25 percent of compensation. Tandem plans had been the industry standard for small, closely held businesses, such as medical practices, that want to accumulate and deduct maximum benefits for owner-employees. In addition to the advantages of administering only a single plan, the mandatory contribution required by the money purchase plan can be eliminated, giving the business the flexibility to reduce contributions during downturns or when funds are needed for other business purposes, such as expansion.

Observation

In addition to the increase in the deduction limit to 25 percent of compensation, the increase in the amount of compensation that may be used to figure allowable contributions ($205,000 in 2004) and the increase in allowable annual additions ($41,000 for 2004) increase deductions for profit-sharing plan contributions. These combined changes allow owners of small, closely held businesses, especially those with few employees, to maximize their plan benefits without the complications of tandem plans. For example, in 2004 a company may deduct a full $41,000 contribution to a profit-sharing plan made on behalf of a higher paid employee (25 percent of up to $205,000 of compensation, but not more than the $41,000 limit on annual additions). Before these liberalizations, by comparison, the maximum deductible contribution in this situation was only $25,500 (15 percent of up to $170,000 of compensation).

Observation

An owner of a small, closely held business whose compensation is less than the $164,000 needed to obtain the maximum $41,000 deduction can increase the contribution through the use of a 401(k) plan. Employee elective deferrals to a 401(k) plan do not count toward the 25 percent of compensation deduction limit.

Impact of Reduced Capital Gains and Dividend Tax Rates

The lowered tax rates on dividends and capital gains compel investors to rethink how they allocate their stocks and bonds between tax-advantaged accounts and taxable accounts. The reduction in tax rates affecting both dividends and capital gains strengthens the case for many investors to hold bonds in their tax-advantaged accounts and to allocate more dividend-paying and capital-gains generating investments to taxable accounts (see Chapter 2 for details).

Observation

These rate reductions, however, should have little impact on the decision whether to participate in 401(k) plans or 403(b) plans. The combination of tax deductions, tax-deferred accumulation, and the potential for employer matching contributions should continue to make these plans the first-choice savings vehicle for retirement (despite the fact that distributions are subject to ordinary tax rates). The only taxpayers who should reconsider plan participation are older taxpayers who are close to retirement, receive no company match, and expect to be in a higher tax bracket later.

(continued)

Continued

Similarly, deductible individual retirement accounts (IRAs), simplified employee pensions (SEPs), and Keoghs should not be impacted by the reduced tax rates for most people. The immediate tax deduction combined with tax-deferred growth continues to provide an attractive after-tax potential (despite the ordinary income tax treatment on distributions). These accounts continue to be particularly attractive for portfolios that produce significant short-term capital gain or ordinary income. (These subjects are discussed in more detail in Chapter 3.)

Medical Coverage Changes

Health Savings Accounts

Health savings accounts (HSAs) are a new way to pay for the high cost of medical care. These are high-deductible health insurance plans combined with savings-type accounts. The funds in the savings-type account can be used to pay medical costs not covered by insurance.

Contributions to HSAs are deductible within limits. Withdrawals after age 65 can be taken for any purpose on a penalty-free basis.

Health Reimbursement Accounts

Employers may contribute fixed amounts each year to employee accounts that can be tapped to pay medical costs not covered by insurance. Neither the contributions nor the withdrawals are taxable to the employee. Unused amounts in the accounts can be carried forward and used in future years.

Flexible Spending Arrangements

Employees may be given the option to use a portion of their compensation to pay their medical costs on a pre-tax basis. Salary reduction amounts they commit to flexible spending arrangements are not subject to income tax. However, currently funds remaining in the FSA at the end of the year are forfeited and cannot be carried forward to the next year.

For details on these medical plans, see Chapter 6.

Estate Tax Changes

The estate tax—and another death tax called the generation-skipping transfer (GST) tax—began to phase out starting in 2002 and will be eliminated entirely in 2010. The gift tax is not repealed, but its effect has been reduced under certain circumstances. As with the income tax provisions, all of the estate and gift tax changes are scheduled to sunset after 2010. Therefore, the repeal of the estate tax will last for only one year (2010) unless Congress makes further changes that are signed into law. Accompanying the repeal of the estate tax are some income tax changes that may cause appreciation in some of a decedent's property to be subject to income tax. Currently, all appreciation in property that occurred during a decedent's life escapes capital gains taxation. These and other changes will cause many people to reconsider and revise their estate plans.

Phase Down of the Estate Tax

The gradual repeal of the estate tax is accomplished by:
- Increasing the amount that is shielded from estate tax.
- Reducing the top estate tax rate.

Exemption Increases

The estate tax exemption amount in 2004 and 2005 is $1.5 million. Thereafter, the exemption amount increases gradually to $3.5 million in 2009 for estate tax purposes. The gift tax exemption amount remains at $1 million. The GST exemption amount is the same as the estate tax exemption amount (e.g., $1.5 million in 2004).

Observation

The annual gift tax exclusion has not been changed by recent tax acts, but is adjusted annually for inflation. For 2004, the limit is $11,000 ($22,000 for couples who agree to split the gift).

Rate Reduction

The highest estate and gift tax rate—which had been 55 percent in 2001—is 48 percent in 2004. It will decline by 1 percent a year to 45 percent in 2007.

Beginning in 2010, the top gift tax rate is scheduled to decline to 35 percent, which is the same as the top individual income tax rate. The estate, GST, and gift tax rates and exemptions, from now through 2011, are represented in Table 1.2 on page 39.

Caution

The increased estate tax exemption requires taxpayers to re-examine their estate plans if their wills and those of their spouses contain *bypass* or *credit-shelter* trusts, which many wills do to ensure that both spouses' estates receive the full estate tax exemption. These bequests are intended to leave the maximum amounts that can be passed on to children or other heirs (or in trusts for their benefits) without incurring estate tax. As the exemption increases, these arrangements will be funded with larger and larger amounts, and possibly all, of a decedent's assets, sometimes leaving nothing outright for the surviving spouse.

	Exemption (in $ Millions)			Highest Estate, GST, and Gift Tax Rate
Year	**Estate Tax**	**GST Tax**	**Gift Tax**	**(%)**
2004	1.5	1.5	1	48
2005	1.5	1.5	1	47
2006	2	2	1	46
2007	2	2	1	45
2008	2	2	1	45
2009	3.5	3.5	1	45
2010	N/A (taxes repealed)	N/A (taxes repealed)	1	35 (Gift tax) 0 (Estate and GST tax)
2011 and later	1	1.12 (indexed)	1	55

Table 1.2   Year-by-Year Transfer Tax Rates and Exemptions

Loss of Credit for State Death Taxes

In the past, federal estate tax could be offset by a credit for state death taxes paid at a decedent's death. The credit could have been approximately 16 percent of the estate. In 2004, however, only 25 percent of the otherwise allowable credit can be claimed. In 2005, the state death tax credit will be repealed and replaced by a deduction for those taxes actually paid to any state.

Observation

The credit has been an important source of revenue for many states. Some states have enacted their own estate taxes to compensate for the repeal of this credit, and others are considering similar actions, a factor that should be considered when people decide where to live in retirement.

Loss of Full Basis Step-Up

Repeal of the estate tax in 2010 will be accompanied by the repeal of the present income tax rules, which provide that a beneficiary's basis (the cost used to figure the gain when property is sold or otherwise disposed of) in assets, acquired from a decedent, is generally "stepped-up" to fair market value as of the date of death. This basis step-up eliminates capital gains tax liability on appreciation in inherited assets that occurred during the decedent's lifetime. Those who inherit property from decedents who die in 2010, however, will receive only a limited basis step-up, which will eliminate income tax on a maximum of $1.3 million of gain that accrued during the decedent's life. Property inherited by a surviving spouse will get an additional $3 million of basis increase, thereby allowing a total basis increase of up to $4.3 million for property transferred to a surviving spouse. (If the decedent was a nonresident alien, the aggregate basis increase would be limited to $60,000, regardless of the beneficiary's relationship to the decedent.)

In addition to the allowable basis step-up, an estate or its beneficiaries who acquire the principal residence of a decedent who dies in 2010 will be able to qualify for tax-free treatment on its sale if that decedent could have qualified. The result can be an additional income tax-free gain of a maximum of $250,000.

The estate's executor will choose which of the decedent's assets will receive the basis increase. (There will be a number of restrictions on basis allocation to avoid the creation of artificial tax losses and other effects not intended by the rule.) Certain additional basis increases will be permitted so that the decedent's losses that were not deducted are not wasted. After permitted basis increases have been exhausted, beneficiaries will receive a basis in the property equal to the decedent's adjusted basis (referred to as a carryover basis) or the fair market value of the property on the date of the decedent's death, whichever is less. For property owned jointly by spouses, only the decedent's half of the property will be eligible for a basis increase.

Donors and estate executors will be required to report information about certain transfers to the IRS and to donees and estate beneficiaries, including basis and holding period information.

Observation

The executor will be responsible for allocating the aggregate basis increase limits among different assets and various beneficiaries of the property. If some beneficiaries receive higher basis property, the other beneficiaries may be burdened with higher capital gains if they sell the inherited property.

Estate planning may help minimize the potential for family strife or litigation over basis allocation issues after a benefactor's death.

Caution

Only property transferred outright to the surviving spouse or held in a special form of trust known as a qualified terminable interest property (QTIP) trust qualifies for the additional $3 million of basis increase for property passing to surviving spouses. Many persons now have testamentary plans in which bequests to surviving spouses are held in other forms of trusts that qualify for the marital deduction for estate tax purposes, but won't qualify for the $3 million basis increase.

Observation

For those interested in charitable giving, retirement assets are an excellent choice of assets to leave to charity. Because retirement assets qualify for a step-up in basis neither before nor after the repeal of the estate tax and, generally, don't even qualify for capital gains rates, income tax consequences can be minimized by leaving the retirement assets rather than other property or cash to charity.

Observation

Presently, retirement and other assets that may not be stepped-up are often left to the surviving spouse rather than to children or other heirs. Starting in 2010, the reverse may be desirable, since there could be a need to use the maximum amount of step-up for post-2010 transfers to a surviving spouse. But this decision is complicated by other considerations: That only a surviving spouse may make certain favorable IRA withdrawal elections is one example. Careful planning is required.

More Conservation Easements Deductible

There is a special estate tax deduction for donations of qualified conservation easements. To claim the deduction, the land does not have to be located within a certain distance of a metropolitan area, national park, wilderness area, or an Urban National Forest as designated by the USDA Forest Service, as had been required in the past. A qualified conservation easement may be claimed for estate tax purposes with respect to any land that is located in the United States or its possessions.

Observation

This liberalization may lead to increased use of this technique, which may be attractive to environmentally minded landowners.

Qualified Domestic Trusts

A qualified domestic trust (QDOT) qualifies for the estate tax marital deduction when the surviving spouse is not a U.S. citizen. Generally, the estate tax is deferred until the death of the surviving spouse, at which time an estate tax based upon the value of the trust principal that remains must be paid. If distributions of trust principal are paid out to the surviving spouse before death, estate tax also would be payable based on the value of those distributions. The QDOT principal escapes estate taxation if the surviving spouse dies in 2010. However, any distribution of principal from a QDOT to a living spouse will remain subject to the estate tax through 2020, but would be free of estate tax in 2021. But because 2021 will occur after the December 31, 2010 sunset date, the 2001 Tax Act in effect, voids this provision.

Observation

It is possible to avoid estate tax entirely in the case of QDOTs that are established before 2010. QDOTs, therefore, should be considered when planning the estate of anyone married to a non-U.S. citizen.

Installment Payment of Estate Taxes

To alleviate the liquidity problems of estates comprised significantly of closely held business interests, qualifying estates may defer the estate tax attributable to the closely held business on an installment basis for up to 14 years at a low interest rate. It is now easier to qualify for installment payment relief. For example, it now applies to certain qualified lending and finance business interests, as well as to certain holding company stock. In addition, the cap on the number of partners that can be included in a partnership or shareholders in a closely held corporation and still be eligible for installment payment relief is 45 owners. To qualify for the installment payment relief, a lending and finance business must meet several technical requirements. In particular, its stock or debt could not have been publicly traded at any time within the three years immediately preceding the decedent's death. Also, an estate relying on the relief for qualified lending or finance businesses under the new law must make the installment payments in 5 years rather than 14. Similarly, an estate taking advantage of the new holding company rules must pay the tax over 9 years.

Observation

This provision provides additional relief for an often overlooked issue of estate planning: ensuring sufficient liquidity to pay estate taxes. By liberalizing the rules, additional businesses can qualify for this relief. However, they must still comprise at least a certain minimum percentage of the total estate assets; other requirements apply as well.

Repeal of Estate Tax Break for Family Businesses

The special estate tax deduction for qualified family owned business interests (QFOBI) can no longer be claimed; it was repealed at the end of 2003.

Observation

This deduction was repealed because the increase in the regular estate tax exemption (discussed above) to $1.5 million in 2004 exceeds the total amount of the qualified family owned business interest deduction, which was limited to $1.3 million, less the estate tax exemption amount. Thus, estates of family owned business owners will not be hurt by the repeal, but will not be entitled to an estate tax exemption any greater than other estates.

What's Next?

In this chapter, we have explained the far-reaching effects of the major tax changes in recent years, shown the importance of planning to adjust for continuing changes, and reviewed the main provisions affecting individuals. Now it is time to discuss in detail how taxpayers should handle their investments to take advantage of new opportunities in light of the current law tax rates on dividends and capital gains. Although people who profit from investments generally must hand over some of their gains to the government in the form of taxes, no one has any obligation to pay any more than is legally due, and it is as wise as it is legitimate to plan an investment strategy to take maximum advantage of what is provided in the tax law.

Chapter 2
INVESTMENTS AND STOCK OPTIONS

During the years 2000 through 2002, investors were more worried about their investment losses rather than the taxes they would have to pay on investment gains. More recently in 2003, the stock market has rebounded. During this time, investors have been rewarded with reduced regular tax rates for interest and short-term gains, and with even lower rates for long-term capital gains and dividends. These changes should attract the attention of every investor, whether they invest in stocks, bonds, sophisticated hedge funds, or simple certificates of deposit. However, the changes are not permanent. The reduced regular tax rates are scheduled to apply only through 2010, and the new capital gains and dividends rates apply only through 2008. Clearly, it is imperative for investors to continuously monitor their portfolios in light of the ever-changing tax regulations in order to maximize their after-tax rate of return.

Under current tax regulations, individual income tax brackets are adjusted for inflation annually. As these adjustments occur, investor tax liability is reduced on investment income subject to ordinary income rates, such as interest and short-term capital gains. Long-term capital gains and dividends are taxed more favorably. They are subject to a maximum tax of only 15 percent. For those in the two lowest tax brackets—such as many children and grandchildren—the rate is a mere 5 percent and, for 2008, it will be zero!

Investors must also consider the effect of the alternative minimum tax (AMT) on any market gains. The after-tax benefit from investing in municipal bonds, for instance, may be lessened for investors who are subject to the AMT. Even though the reduced capital gains and dividends tax rates apply for AMT as well as regular income tax purposes, these types of income can nonetheless help trigger the AMT. There is modest relief from the AMT through 2004, which was increased by the 2003 Tax Act, but after that the tax reverts to its terms before the cut—a fact that investors should keep in mind in planning for 2005 and beyond. Even before 2005, many upper income taxpayers will feel AMT's sting. Congress's Joint Committee on Taxation estimates that 2.9 million taxpayers will be subject to the AMT in 2004. The general consensus is that Washington will have to come up with a more permanent solution to the AMT problem or suffer the political consequences. However, the increasing budget deficits will make finding a solution elusive.

Instead of investing in municipal bonds, many taxpayers will choose to convert some of their investments to Coverdell Education Savings Accounts or college tuition savings plans for their children. Others may find that the reduced tax rates on investment income favor other saving strategies. We describe these strategies in depth in Chapter 5.

Investors should also take note that the phasing out of the estate tax has a "Catch-22" clause that should impact their investment decisions: In 2010, securities and other capital assets held in an estate at death will no longer escape all capital gains tax when passed on to heirs. Under the new law, the heirs' tax-free gains on inherited property will be limited to a *total* of $1.3 million. An additional $3 million of gains on property received by a surviving spouse will also escape capital gains tax. Until now, many investors have assumed that securities with very large gains should be retained until death for heirs in order to receive a tax-free step up in basis. In some instances, that strategy may not be appropriate as a result of the limit on capital gains that can pass to heirs tax-free in 2010.

In this chapter, we discuss in detail the many ways you can maximize your investment options on an after-tax basis under today's tax regulations. Particular attention is paid to making the best tax use of capital losses. We include a checklist of ideas to consider as you plan your investment strategies for the decade to come.

Capital Gains

Capital gain income results when a taxpayer sells or exchanges a capital asset that is held for longer than one year. Examples of capital assets include shares of stock or securities, a personal residence, or a work of art.

Favorable Rates

The rate on long-term capital gains (gains from assets held for more than one year) is currently only 15 percent.

Example

In April 2004, an individual in the top ordinary income tax bracket (35 percent in 2003) sold stock that he purchased over a year earlier, recognizing a gain of $10,000. His long-term capital gains tax is $1,500—15 percent of $10,000.

Observation

The reduced tax rates on long-term capital gains make stock investments more advantageous over shorter holding periods and reduces the attractiveness of "ordinary income" investments, such as regular IRAs (but not Roth IRAs), tax-deferred annuities, and fixed income investments.

Observation

The capital gains rate for taxpayers in high tax brackets was effectively increased by the itemized deduction cutback and the personal exemption phase-out (see Chapter 8). The loss of personal exemptions and phase out of itemized deductions will be less of a problem in the future, when the phase-outs of these write-offs are gradually reduced, beginning in 2006. For now, the marginal tax rate on net long-term capital gains for higher income taxpayers may be 22 percent or higher, depending on personal circumstances.

Exceptions to the 15 Percent Rate

Individuals in the 10 percent or 15 percent ordinary income tax bracket have a long-term capital gains rate of only 5 percent. For sales in 2008, there is no tax on these gains.

Example

Assume your 19-year-old daughter's regular income (from wages and interest) is taxed at no more than 15 percent, and she sells stock that she purchased over a year ago for a gain of $10,000. Her capital gains tax is only $500 (5 percent of $10,000).

Observation

The availability of the 5 percent rate for those in the lowest two tax brackets presents a great family income-splitting opportunity. A higher income tax bracket parent can transfer stock or other capital assets held to their lower income tax bracket children or grandchildren. The children or grandchildren, in turn, can turn around and sell the assets (but not before the year they turn 14 or the "kiddie tax" will kick in) and qualify for the lower 5 percent rate to the extent the gains do not push their income above the 15 percent bracket (taxable income of $29,050 for singles in 2004). The holding period for the asset transferred carries over to recipients of the property when the gift is made. As a result, the transfer results in a 10-percentage-point tax savings.

Example

An individual in the top tax bracket (35 percent in 2004) owns stock purchased more than one year ago on which he has a $10,000 gain. If he sold the stock in 2004 to help pay his grandson's college tuition, for example, his long-term capital gains tax would be $1,500 or 15 percent of $10,000. If he gives the stock to his 17-year-old grandson, who has only a few thousand dollars of taxable income this year from a summer job, the tax bill would be only $500 on his grandson's sale of the stock, saving $1,000.

A higher maximum tax rate of 28 percent applies to long-term capital gains from the sale of collectibles (such as art or antiques) and to one-half of the long-term capital gains from the sale of qualified small-business stock (the other half of the gain on the sale of such stock, up to certain limits, is tax-free). Furthermore, there is a 25 percent tax rate on part of the gain resulting from the sale of real estate where depreciation deductions were previously taken.

Example

An individual who is not an art dealer sells an oil painting from his personal collection, which he has owned for many years, for $100,000 more than he paid for it. His capital gains tax liability is $28,000 or 28 percent of $100,000.

> **Observation**
>
> The 15 percent rate on long-term capital gains and dividends is set to run only through 2008, so investors with unrecognized gains may want to evaluate selling assets now in order to take advantage of the current low rate. Of course, investors will want to compare the prospective tax savings to the future appreciation potential for the investment before making any decision.

No More Advantage for Five-Year Gains

There has always been a required minimum holding period to qualify for long-term capital gains rates. Over the years, it has varied from more than six months to more than two years. Before May 7, 2003, there was a separate holding period for special capital gains rates. The rate was 18 percent (or 8 percent for those in the two lowest tax brackets) for certain capital assets held more than five years:

- **18 percent rate.** This rate would have applied to sales of property held for more than five years if the holding period for the property began in 2001 or later.

- **8 percent rate.** This rate would have applied to sales of property held for more than five years and sold in 2001 or later. There was no requirement for the holding period to have begun after 2001 to qualify for this low rate, however.

These special rates have been repealed for now. However, they should not be completely forgotten since they may come into play after 2008, when the current low capital gains rates expire.

Effect of Past Election to Get the 18 Percent Rate

Investors had the opportunity to qualify assets purchased before 2001 for the 18 percent rate by electing to treat any or all of the assets as having been sold and repurchased at the beginning of 2001. Those who made this election for readily tradable stock were deemed to have sold and repurchased it at its closing price on the first business day after January 1, 2001. The deemed sale and repurchase of other capital assets, such as real estate or artwork, was treated as made at their fair market values on January 1, 2001. By making this election, investors were able to start a new post-2000 holding period without actually going through the trouble and expense of selling and repurchasing the property.

Caution

If you made a deemed-sale election, it *cannot* be revoked even though long-term capital gains rates have now dropped to 15 percent. Congress did not elect to allow those who previously made the election, and as a result prepaid capital gains tax at a higher rate, to go back and undo it in order to take advantage of the new 15 percent rate.

Netting Rules

Favorable capital gains rates and the long-term capital gains holding requirements may influence the decision as to when a property is sold, which in turn, effects the tax that is ultimately paid. When calculating capital gains income, keep in mind that the following ordering rules apply to netting capital gains and losses. The rules are fairly complicated, but they generally produce the lowest overall tax.

Long-term capital gains and losses (for this purpose, long-term refers to a holding period of more than one year) are divided into three groups determined by tax rates:

1. A 28 percent group (for long-term capital gains from the sale of collectibles, such as art or antiques, and half of the long-term capital gains from the sale of qualified small-business stock).

2. A 25 percent group (for part of the gain from the sale of depreciable real estate).

3. A 15 percent group for all other capital assets.

For those in the two lowest ordinary income tax brackets, gains and losses in the 5 percent, 8 percent, and 10 percent groups also must be netted. Long-term gains and losses within a tax-rate group are first netted against one another. Net losses within a long-term tax-rate group then are used to offset net gains from the long-term tax-rate group with the highest tax rate. If there are net losses remaining, they offset gains from the next highest tax-rate group.

Example

Assume that for 2004 there will be net losses in the 15 percent tax-rate group. The net losses first offset any net gains in the 28 percent tax-rate group, then offset net gains in the 25 percent tax-rate group, and finally, offset net gains in the 15 percent tax-rate group. This automatically produces maximum tax savings from the losses. Similarly, long-term capital loss carryovers offset net gains for the highest long-term tax-rate group first, then the other long-term tax rate groups in descending order.

Example

A net long-term capital loss carryover from 2003 first offsets 2004 net 28 percent capital gains, then net 25 percent capital gains, finally, net 15 percent gains.

Net short-term capital losses offset net long-term capital gains beginning with the highest tax-rate group.

Example

A net short-term capital loss first offsets net 28 percent capital gains, then net 25 percent capital gains, and, finally, net 15 percent capital gains.

Net long-term capital losses can offset short-term capital gains.

Capital Losses

Capital losses are deductible dollar-for-dollar against capital gains. In addition, you may deduct up to $3,000 in net capital losses (either short-term or long-term) each year against ordinary income (such as wages or interest income). Amounts in excess of $3,000 may be carried forward indefinitely.

Wash Sale Rule

If securities or mutual funds held have significantly declined in value and a recovery in price is not anticipated in the near future, consideration should be given to selling the securities or funds currently to take advantage of the loss. For investment reasons, there may be an ongoing desire to maintain a similar type of investment. The repurchase must be made carefully, however, so as to not immediately repurchase the same or "substantially identical" (the IRS uses this term to broaden the prohibited repurchase to securities and/or mutual funds that are not identical to what you had sold, but are essentially the same) assets. Tax wash sale rules prevent you from recognizing the tax loss if the repurchase occurs within 31 days of the sale for the same or substantially the same security.

If the wash sale rule is triggered, the resulting loss is suspended and added to the cost basis (the amount you pay for the security plus other acquisition costs, such as brokerage commissions). When the replacement security is sold, the suspended amount will reduce the taxable gain or increase the taxable loss.

To avoid the wash sale rule, you must either avoid purchasing the same or substantially identical assets within the 31-day period, or buy the same or "substantially identical" assets at least 31 days before or after the sale of the securities or mutual funds. Of course, the latter alternative involves substantial investment risk as the market can move against the targeted strategy in the 31-day period.

Caution

Be careful not to trigger the wash sale rule unintentionally. A wash sale will happen, for example, if you sell *part* of your investment in a security or fund at a loss, and a dividend paid on the remaining shares is automatically reinvested in the same shares within the restricted 31-day period.

Observation

It is always helpful to review your realized and unrealized capital gains and losses as well as loss carryovers on a periodic basis. This is especially important for future tax planning. If you have unrealized capital losses, consider recognizing losses to the extent of realized capital gains if also prudent from an investment perspective. Also, you may wish to realize an additional $3,000 in losses since the incremental amount can be used to offset taxable ordinary income.

Protecting and Postponing Stock Gains

Current regulations prevent the use of the "short-against-the-box" technique to safely lock in gains while postponing the taxable recognition that would occur upon the sale. Two other viable strategies remain:

1. **Buying put options covering stock you own.** A put option entitles the holder to sell a number of shares (usually in lots of

100 shares) of the underlying security at a stated price on or before a fixed expiration date. By purchasing an option to sell a security at a fixed price, any decline in the price of the security is likely to be offset, at least in part, by an increase in the price of the put option purchased.

2. **Writing covered call options.** A call option entitles the holder to purchase a number of shares of the underlying security at a stated price on or before a fixed expiration date. When a call is written, the seller of the call option receives money today in exchange for agreeing to purchase the security back at the call price in the future. As a result, the holder of a security who writes a call option on the security protects their position to some extent by the proceeds from the sale of the option. More complex strategies also exist, including collars and variable pre-paid forwards. Additionally, by using a charitable remainder trust, capital gains can also be deferred or possibly eliminated.

Observation

The lower tax rate on capital gains should cause you to review your stock-hedging strategies. Carrying costs associated with hedging strategies that were acceptable with a 20 percent capital gains rate may be excessive with a 15 percent capital gains rate. At some point, it may make sense for you simply to pay the capital gains tax and unwind the hedging strategy. This could be particularly true for grandfathered short-against-the-box transactions where the underlying security has continued to appreciate.

Passive Activity Losses

Investment losses are limited by a complex set of provisions known as the *passive activity loss rules*. In general, losses and credits from passive activities can offset only passive income and may not be used against earned income (such as salaries) or portfolio income (such as dividends or interest). Passive activities generally include any business or investment activity in which you do not materially participate. For example, a rental property is usually considered as a passive activity.

> ### Observation
> Real estate professionals may deduct losses and credits from rental real estate activities in which they materially participate.

Consider the following year-end strategies if you have unusable passive losses:

- Purchase investments that generate passive income, to the extent the purchase is consistent with your overall investment strategy.
- Become a material participant in the activity, if feasible, by increasing your level of involvement.
- Sell or dispose of your entire interest in the passive activity to free up the losses.

> ### Observation
> Even more restrictive rules apply to certain types of passive activities, such as publicly traded partnerships. Publicly traded partnership losses can offset only publicly traded partnership income, not income from other types of passive activities.

Careful Record Keeping: Identification of Securities

If you hold many securities, it is imperative to keep accurate records of your purchase history in order to maximize the tax savings at the time of sale. Because of differences in holding periods and the tax basis of individual lots, a sale can trigger a short-term or long-term gain or loss, depending on which securities are sold or are deemed to have been sold. Accurate record keeping is critical to minimizing taxes. If you redeem an actual security certificate at the time of sale, the securities sold will be those identified on the certificate. If one certificate represents securities acquired on different dates or at different prices, the specific securities to be sold can be identified to the executing broker in writing. If you do not identify specific securities, you will generally be deemed to have sold the first securities acquired, which would have the longest holding period (and therefore might be taxed at a lower rate), but may also have the largest taxable gain.

Observation

Mutual fund shares are usually treated in the same way as other securities, or you can use their average cost when determining basis. Once you apply the earliest-cost or average-cost method to a mutual fund, you must continue to use that method in future years.

Observation

When selling stock that has risen in value, taxes can be reduced by identifying the securities with the highest basis as the ones that are being sold. However, if the securities have been held for one year or less, any gain will be short-term, subject to tax at ordinary income rates.

Dividends

Dividends received by an individual shareholder from domestic and many foreign corporations (including American Depository Receipts or ADRs) that meet the definition of "qualified dividend income" are taxed at the same low rates that apply to long-term capital gains.

This treatment applies for purposes of both the regular tax and the AMT. Thus, qualified dividends are taxed at rates of 5 percent (zero, in 2008) for taxpayers in the two lowest tax brackets, and at 15 percent for those whose income is taxed above the 15 percent tax bracket. Qualified dividend income passed through to individuals from partnerships, S corporations, limited liability companies, and trusts maintains its character as qualified dividend income and thus is taxed to individuals at the new reduced rates.

Caution

Similar to taxpayers who have been subject to AMT in the past due to high capital gains, taxpayers who now receive large amounts of dividend as well as capital gain income may find themselves subject to AMT. Taxpayers in the 28 percent, 33 percent, or 35 percent marginal tax bracket who receive dividend income may find themselves subject to the AMT due to the disparity in the rates between the AMT and the regular tax. For example, a taxpayer in the 35 percent tax bracket with $1 of dividend income would save $0.20 for regular tax purposes (35 percent versus 15 percent tax rate), but only $0.13 for AMT purposes (28 percent versus 15 percent tax rate). Further, the phase-out of the AMT exemption results in AMT income effectively being taxed at 125 percent of the applicable AMT rate. Thus, it is possible that a taxpayer in the AMT phase-out range will pay an effective rate of 22 percent on capital gains and dividends rather than the stated AMT rate of 15 percent (15 percent plus 25 percent of 28 percent).

A shareowner must hold dividend-paying stock for more than 60 days during the 121-day period beginning 60 days before the ex-dividend date in order for the dividends received on the stock to be eligible for the reduced tax rates. For dividends received on certain preferred stock (generally dividends that represent an earnings period of more than one year), shareholders must hold the stock for more than 90 days during the 181-day period beginning 90 days before the ex-dividend date. These required holding periods do not include any days on which the taxpayer has reduced the risk of loss on the stock by purchasing a put, selling a call (other than a qualified covered call), executing a short sale of the stock, or having entered into a cashless collar or prepaid variable forward contract. Additionally, a taxpayer who is under an obligation to pay the dividend to another party will not receive qualified dividend income. Thus, a person with a short-against-the-box position will pay tax at ordinary rates on dividends received.

If an individual receives an extraordinary dividend eligible for the reduced rates, any loss on the sale of the dividend-paying stock is treated as a long-term capital loss to the extent of the dividend. (A dividend on preferred stock is treated as extraordinary if it equals 5 or more percent of the shareholder's adjusted basis in the preferred stock; a dividend on common stock is treated as extraordinary if it equals 10 percent or more of the shareholder's adjusted basis in the common stock.) Clearly, these rules make it more difficult for taxpayers to convert short-term capital gains into dividend income taxed at lower rates. However, taxpayers who have short-term capital gains, and no potential long-term capital gains or losses, could use extraordinary dividends to avoid the higher tax on short-term capital gains. The taxpayers would still have to meet the holding period requirements described earlier.

Mutual Funds and REITs

Mutual funds generally are able to pass through qualified dividend income received to the fund's shareholders where the qualified dividend will be taxed at the reduced rates. However, other types of income received by a mutual fund, such as interest received on notes or bonds, or short-term capital gain, are not qualified dividend income, even though the payments are made to mutual fund shareholders in the form of a dividend. Therefore, money market fund dividends, which represent interest earned by the money market fund, are not qualified dividend income.

Dividends paid by a real estate investment trust (REIT) generally are not eligible for the reduced dividend rates. However, dividends received by a REIT shareholder will be considered qualified dividend income to the extent that the REIT had net taxable income in the preceding year.

Observation

Mutual funds and REITs will advise shareholders as to whether the distributions are qualified dividend income eligible for the reduced tax rates.

Preferred Stock

Whether dividends on preferred stock qualify for the reduced dividend tax rates depends on the classification of the preferred stock. If the preferred stock pays a dividend from corporate earnings and profits, and the preferred stock is considered a stock, the dividend will be taxed at no more than 15 percent. But if the preferred stock is considered a debt instrument, its "dividend" will continue to be taxed at ordinary income rates. Since many preferred stocks are bonds in disguise, their dividends will not be eligible for the 15 percent rate.

Observation

It is expected that companies will begin issuing preferred stock that conforms to the new regulations in order to capitalize on the demand for the preferred tax treatment.

Impact on Short Sales

A short sale is the sale of a security currently that is not owned. When a dividend is paid on stock that has been shorted before the date the short sale is closed, the short seller must pay to the lender of the shares an equivalent amount in lieu of that dividend. In general, these "in lieu of" payments are treated as interest paid for the use of the property borrowed for use in the short sale.

Once the borrowed stock or securities have been sold pursuant to a short sale, neither the short seller nor the lender retains any ownership interest in the stock, therefore, the "in lieu of dividend" payment made to the lender of the stock by the seller is not a "dividend" in the sense of being a distribution made by the corporation with respect to its stock. As such, "in lieu of dividend" payments do not qualify for the reduced rates.

Impact on Margin Accounts

In the past, investors may not have known or cared whether their stock was borrowed and they were receiving "in lieu of dividend" payments rather than actual dividends. Now, however, if a dividend is considered an "in lieu of dividend" payment, the lower dividend tax rates will not be available. As a result, margin accounts may become less popular in the future since most agreements governing margin accounts specifically allow for the borrowing of shares held in a margin account.

Observation

Borrowing dividend-paying stock for short sales may become more expensive since taxable lenders will expect to be compensated for the loss of the lower dividend tax rates.

Impact on Foreign Tax Credit

Special rules apply in determining a taxpayer's foreign tax credit limitation for qualified dividend income. Because qualified dividends now receive preferential tax treatment in the United States, dividends taxed overseas will need to be adjusted accordingly when computing the foreign tax credit.

Impact of Reduced Tax Rates on Investment Allocation

An investor's asset allocation should be revisited in light of the current low rates on qualified dividends and capital gains including the decision as to what investments should be in which type of account, either a taxable or tax-deferred account. There is no simple answer as to which investment is the most beneficial in each type of account. Clearly, consideration should be given as to the character of the expected return produced by the investment—short or long-term capital gain, nontaxable or taxable ordinary income, the expected portfolio turnover, the expected return on the asset class, and the time period of tax deferral.

Historically, investments producing significant amounts of taxable income each year (taxable interest or dividends, short-term capital gains, or ordinary income) would have primarily been allocated first to tax-deferred or tax-free accounts. So too would investment styles with significant portfolio turnover. Additionally, long-term capital gain assets with little portfolio turnover would have primarily been allocated first to taxable accounts.

Now, taxpayers with long-term tax deferral opportunities may be well advised to put their highest potential earning assets in tax-deferred accounts even if the withdrawal will be taxed at a rate much higher than the 15 percent current tax rate. Tax-deferred compounding on high-growth-rate asset categories for long periods of time can more than offset the benefits of low current tax rates.

Taxpayers with shorter term tax-deferral opportunities generally should place more emphasis on the current tax rates (and tax efficiencies) when making asset allocation decisions. Shorter periods of tax deferral may not justify the loss of lower rate earnings.

Tax-Exempt and Taxable Bonds

Most interest earned on bonds is subject to tax at ordinary income rates. In most interest rate environments, bonds paying tax-exempt interest are only appropriate for investors in higher income tax brackets (federal and state). However, depending on the date on which the bond matures and the current market conditions, some long-term municipal bonds may produce a higher after-tax yield even in the 15 percent bracket (see Chapter 8). The decision is driven by the interest rate differential between taxable and tax-free bonds, assuming similar maturity and credit quality. It is important to take into account the state tax implications as well. Most tax-exempt bonds issued by a state, or a political subdivision of a state, other than the state of residence, subject the taxpayer to state income tax even though the interest is free from federal tax.

Observation

Lower tax rates impact the relationship between tax-exempt and taxable bonds and will reduce the attractiveness of tax-exempt bonds, everything else being equal. Recently, since the federal tax rates have declined and tax brackets have been adjusted upwards for inflation, allowing more income to be earned without pushing a taxpayer into a higher tax bracket, tax-exempt bond issuers are being forced to raise the interest rate on their bonds to remain competitive with similar quality taxable bonds.

Taxable "Tax-Exempt" Bonds

Certain bonds (private activity bonds) are tax-exempt for regular income tax purposes but are taxable for the AMT. As a result, the private activity bonds typically carry a slightly higher interest rate than bonds that are exempt from both regular tax and the AMT.

Observation

The demand for private activity municipal bonds should decrease going forward since many more taxpayers are now subject to the AMT.

Observation

If it is unlikely that you will be subject to the AMT now or in the future, you should consider investing in private activity bonds in order to obtain the higher interest rate.

Caution

Just because you may not have been subject to the AMT in the past, you should not assume that you will not be subject to the AMT in future years. Unlike regular income tax rates, AMT rate brackets and exemption amounts are not indexed annually for inflation. AMT liability has been affecting more and more taxpayers. In 2004, AMT relief has been provided in the form of slightly increased exemption amounts. This increased exemption amount, however, is only temporary (see Chapter 1 for details).

Legislative Alert

Congress may continue higher AMT exemption amounts and/or permit certain personal credits to offset AMT liability.

Bond Premium or Discount

Investors who pay more than face value to purchase a bond are said to have purchased the bond at a premium. Bonds purchased at a premium usually carry a higher rate of interest at the time of purchase than the prevailing rate for newly issued comparable bonds. Taxpayers who own bonds purchased at a premium must amortize the premium of a tax-exempt bond by reducing its basis over time, although for taxable bonds, you can elect to amortize the premium by offsetting the premium against the bond's interest. If you elect to amortize the bond premium, you must do so for all bonds owned currently and later acquired. If the premium is not amortized over the bond's life, a loss will typically result when you sell or redeem the bond.

If a bond is issued at a discount from its original issuer, the difference between the issue price and the redemption price (called "original issue discount," or OID) is considered interest income. In almost all cases, a portion of this interest must be included in income each year even though the income is not received until the bond is redeemed. Taxable OID bonds, therefore, are best suited for purchase in tax-deferred accounts, such as IRA or 401(k) accounts, or tax-exempt accounts, such as Roth IRAs.

The original issue discount rules do not apply to U.S. savings bonds, notes that mature in one year or less, or tax-exempt bonds (unless the bonds have been stripped of their coupons). If a taxable bond is purchased with a market discount—that is, a bond that has lost value since its issue date (usually because interest rates have risen since the time of issue)—the resulting gain on sale will, in most cases, be considered interest income to the extent of the accrued market discount. The market discount must be accrued and recognized as ordinary income upon sale. If the bond is sold at a price in excess of the accrued discount, the excess is capital gain. Unlike the rule for taxable bonds, all of the market discount on municipal bonds is treated as ordinary income to the extent of the gain on the disposition of the municipal bond.

Florida Intangibles Trust

If you are a Florida resident and pay a significant amount of Florida intangibles tax each year, you should consider establishing a Florida Intangibles Trust or other vehicle that may exempt from the tax the value of your intangible assets. Note that the tax rate for the Florida intangibles tax has been reduced significantly in the past few years, and now is imposed at the rate of only 0.1 percent ($1 per $1,000 of intangible assets subject to the tax).

> ### *Observation*
> Include the cost of establishing and operating a Florida Intangible Trust or other vehicle when determining whether this type of strategy makes sense for you.

Nonqualified Stock Options

Nonqualified stock options generate compensation income at the time when the options are exercised. The compensation income equals the difference between the fair market value of the stock at the time of exercise and the exercise price. Subsequent appreciation in the value of the stock is taxed at favorable capital gains rates. Most individuals benefit by exercising nonqualified stock options shortly before the options expire, subject to the normal market risk associated with any investment decision. Early exercise at or near the strike price eliminates the downside protection afforded by stock options. By holding off on exercise until the latest point possible, you will benefit from the presumably increased stock value without actually making a cash investment in the stock.

However, if the appreciation potential of the stock is expected to be great, early exercise can be advantageous because it minimizes the portion of the gain that will be taxed as compensation (at ordinary income rates) and maximizes the amount that will qualify for capital gains rates. The decision about when to exercise options should also take into account the amount of appreciation to date, the future prospects of the company, and, most importantly, your unique tax and investment position. Some option plans permit you to pay the exercise price in the form of existing shares, thereby eliminating the need to fund the exercise with cash.

Withholding of federal income tax, Social Security, Medicare, and state and local taxes are all due when the options are exercised. If the stock option is exercised and then sold quickly, the cash generated from the sale can be used to help satisfy these withholding obligations.

Observation

If you intend to retain all of the stock obtained via the exercise of options, it is important to plan properly as to how to satisfy these withholding obligations. Some plans allow the use of shares to cover withholding taxes. Some employers grant "phantom" stock in connection with nonqualified options, which can help cover withholding taxes.

Incentive Stock Options

The new, lower long-term capital gains tax rates make incentive stock options more attractive. However, careful planning is needed to maximize the benefits of incentive stock options if the AMT is a concern.

For regular tax purposes, an incentive stock option (ISO) exercise is not a taxable event (state and local tax treatment may differ). However, at exercise, the difference between the fair market value of the stock on the date of the exercise and the exercise price is added to an individual's alternative minimum taxable income for the purpose of computing the AMT. Additionally, ISOs are not subject to payroll taxes at the time of exercise like nonqualified stock options. The IRS' recent attempt to collect FICA tax on ISO exercise was met with substantial resistance.

ISOs are subject to a number of requirements imposed by the Tax Code that do not apply to nonqualified stock options. For example:

- ISOs cannot be issued at a strike price lower than the value of the stock on the date the options are granted.
- ISOs cannot be exercised more than 10 years after the options are granted.
- ISOs are not transferable except at death and, during the grantee's lifetime, may be exercised only by the grantee.
- ISOs must be exercised within 90 days of termination of employment in order to retain the ISO status.
- There is a $100,000 annual limit on ISO grants.
- In order to obtain favorable ISO tax treatment, the ISO stock cannot be sold within a year of option exercise or within two years of the option grant. If option stock is sold before either of these two periods has expired, the option is treated as a nonqualified option, usually resulting in compensation income to the option holder.

Observation

For taxpayers not otherwise subject to the AMT, ISO exercises should generally be timed to occur over the life of the option (usually 10 years) in order to minimize the AMT impact and to commence the one-year holding period needed to qualify for the 15 percent capital gains tax rate. If little or no planning goes into an ISO exercise, a taxpayer may be required to pay taxes earlier or in larger amounts than may be necessary.

Caution

Care should also be taken not to sell or otherwise dispose of the stock received from an ISO exercise before one year from the exercise date or two years from the grant date, whichever is later. If a sale or disposition occurs prior to one year from the exercise date or two years from the date of grant, the sale will be taxed at ordinary income rates.

Observation

Generally, it is best to exercise ISOs early in the year if the AMT is likely to be paid. The early exercise provides flexibility to sell the shares before year-end and avoid the AMT if the stock drops in value. In this case, the taxpayer will only pay ordinary income tax on the actual gain, rather than the AMT on the spread between the fair market value at exercise and the exercise price.

Idea Checklist

☑ Reevaluate your asset allocation and whether higher return, tax efficient assets should be placed in taxable or tax-deferred accounts. However, keep tax considerations secondary to investment fundamentals.

☑ Consider how reduced capital gains and dividend rates affect investment allocations among your taxable and tax-deferred accounts.

☑ Make gifts of capital assets to your low-income tax bracket children or grandchildren to take advantage of capital gains being subject to tax at only 5 percent (zero percent if not sold until 2008).

☑ Review your capital gains and capital loss positions before year-end. Try to offset capital gains with capital losses. Keep in mind the 30-day wash sale rule.

☑ Consider reallocating some of your bond portfolio to dividend paying stock now that dividends are taxed at no more than 15 percent. Again, keep the tax considerations secondary to investment fundamentals.

☑ Make full use of $3,000 in capital loss deduction that can be used to offset your ordinary income.

☑ Determine whether tax-exempt bonds are an appropriate investment. If so, consider whether investing in "taxable" tax-exempts will improve your cash yield.

☑ Florida residents should consider ways to reduce their Florida intangibles tax liability.

☑ Executives with incentive stock options should consider how, if possible, to minimize AMT on their exercise, and should hold the shares for more than one year (and two years from option grant) to ensure qualifying their gain for the 15 percent capital gains rate.

☑ Consider whether the carrying costs associated with hedging strategies that were acceptable with a 20 percent capital gains rate are still viable with a 15 percent capital gains rate.

☑ A key goal for most investment strategies is to accumulate funds for retirement. Chapter 3 assesses the many ways in which the tax law provides incentives for retirement savings.

Chapter 3
RETIREMENT PLANNING

Today, most workers have much greater tax incentives to save for retirement than ever before. There are much more favorable rules for traditional IRAs, Roth IRAs, Keoghs, and corporate retirement plans. Those who can take advantage of these opportunities can lower their taxes now while helping to ensure their comfort and financial security during retirement. The improvements are particularly welcome now because individual retirement planning is more important than ever. With employer-paid pensions becoming rarer every year and more businesses downsizing, wage earners face the prospect of financing more of their retirement with their own resources. For most people, retirement income is likely to come from three sources:

1. Tax-favored retirement plans, perhaps including defined benefit pension plans, but more likely profit-sharing, stock bonus, IRA and Roth IRA, and employer-sponsored savings plans. These include 401(k), 403(b) (for teachers and employees of tax-exempt organizations), simplified employee pension (SEP) and Keogh plans (for the self-employed), savings incentive match plans for employees (SIMPLE; plans for workers in firms with fewer than 100 employees), and 457 plans for government employees.

2. A taxpayer's investments outside of tax-favored retirement plans.

3. Social Security.

Taxpayers can now increase their contributions to qualified savings plans, with workers age 50 and over permitted to make even more generous catch-up contributions reaching, in some cases, as much as $5,000 a year by 2006. High-income employees who don't qualify for Roth IRAs will be able to enroll in an employer-sponsored Roth incentive savings plan, to which they contribute after-tax funds, but are allowed to withdraw the money and its gains tax-free with no fixed schedule of required lifetime distributions. (Roth funds can even be left income tax-free to an heir.) Employer-matching contributions vest—that is, become nonforfeitable—more rapidly, and the retirement plans will be more portable, allowing workers more easily to transfer the funds when they change jobs. Some lower-income workers can even get a tax credit for as much as 50 percent of the money they contribute to qualified retirement plans and IRAs, which reduces their taxes for the year of the contribution. Especially now that capital gains rates have dropped to 15 percent (at least through 2008), taxpayers must keep in mind the benefits of capital gains tax breaks when planning for retirement. Retirement plans allow tax-free compounding of profits, but almost all payouts are taxed at ordinary income tax rates in the year they are received. Those who expect relatively high income in retirement should weigh the merits of forgoing the tax deferral, investing after-tax funds for retirement and being taxed on sale at lower capital gains rates.

However, they should not forget that the alternative minimum tax (AMT) could void much of the advantage. While capital gains, themselves, are not subject to AMT, they can push total income into the AMT range, subjecting other income and deductions to the AMT.

Observation

Some studies have shown that lower-income individuals may actually pay more tax and have less money available to spend in retirement by contributing to 401(k) or other retirement plans. Part of the reason for this is the high marginal tax rate on social security income for moderate-income taxpayers (see page 100).

We believe that moderate-income taxpayers should use retirement plans and/or IRAs to save for retirement for the following reasons:

• Putting money aside in a retirement plan clearly segregates and identifies the funds for retirement, thus reducing the temptation to spend the funds for other purposes. Indeed, the penalties for early withdrawal and, in some cases, the unavailability of the funds make it more difficult to use the funds prematurely.

• Many 401(k) plans have some portion of the employee contribution matched by the employer. The match is not available for savings outside of the plan.

• While current tax law may, under some circumstances, result in higher taxes at retirement for tax-deferred plan proceeds, it is difficult to predict personal circumstances many years in the future and even more difficult to predict the applicable tax law.

Since most people will benefit from maximizing tax deferral on retirement savings, this chapter details valuable planning techniques and offers suggestions that can help to reduce overall tax bills and maximize income during retirement.

Employer Plans

Qualified Retirement Plans

When possible, you should think about participating in a qualified employer pension or profit-sharing plan, 401(k) plan, 403(b) plan, Keogh, or simplified employee pension (SEP) plan. Qualified plans must meet complex participation, coverage, and nondiscrimination requirements, allowing sponsoring employers to immediately deduct their contributions. Employer contributions on your behalf are not taxed to you until you receive them. Your contributions to these plans reduce your adjusted gross income (AGI) within specified limits as well as your current tax bill. This tax deferral is achieved in exchange for reduced liquidity because you give up immediate access to the funds. However, some plans permit you to borrow up to specified allowable limits from your account, which gives you access to some of your savings if necessary. Even owner-employees, such as sole proprietors, partners, and S corporation shareholders, now may borrow from their retirement plans in the same way that other employees can, without getting hit with the prohibitive excise tax that previously applied.

Observation

The savings incentive match plan for employees (SIMPLE) is available to employees of companies with 100 or fewer employees who do not have other types of retirement plans. Under this type of plan, employees may defer up to $9,000 for 2004 (or $10,500 if age 50 or older by year end). Employers that offer a SIMPLE generally must make a nonelective or matching contribution on behalf of each plan participant.

Observation

There is no longer a "combined plan limit," which in the past put a cap on contributions for highly compensated employees who participate in both an employer's pension plan and a profit-sharing plan. Now, even if you are highly compensated, you can accumulate larger qualified retirement plan benefits.

There are two basic kinds of qualified employer retirement plans:

1. Defined contribution plans.
2. Defined benefit plans.

Defined Contribution Plans

A defined contribution plan allows your company or you—or your company and you—to contribute a set amount each year to the plan. Contributions are set aside in an account for you and are invested on your behalf. Sometimes you have the right to determine how the contributions are invested. With a defined contribution plan, you are not guaranteed a set amount of benefits when you retire. Instead, you receive the amount in the account, which depends on how much was contributed to it and how successfully the funds were invested over the years. You get a periodic statement advising you of your current account balance.

Defined contribution plan benefits are portable, so if you change jobs, you can transfer your vested benefits to an IRA or possibly to your new employer's plan. Most defined benefit pension plans, on the contrary, don't make your vested benefit available before you reach retirement age, unless your benefit is very small (in which case, the plan may cash you out).

The most common defined contribution plans are profit-sharing plans, 401(k) plans, stock bonus plans, money purchase pension plans, and employee stock ownership plans.

Bigger Contributions Allowed

The contribution limit for 2004 is the lesser of 100 percent of compensation or $42,000. This limit will be adjusted annually for inflation. The limit on compensation taken into account in figuring is $210,000, which is also adjusted annually for inflation. The higher limit means that larger contributions and benefits are possible for the more highly compensated.

Caution

Highly paid employees may still not be allowed to take full advantage of the increased contribution limits after nondiscrimination tests are applied.

> ### Observation
> While the 100 percent limit permits allocation to an individual
> account of the entire salary, the 25 percent limitation on de-
> ductions for all contributions (except elective deferrals) will
> apply to prevent a sole proprietor or a one-employee corpora-
> tion from contributing 100 percent.

Profit-Sharing Plans

Profit-sharing plans allow employees to share in the company's
profits, usually through an employer contribution that is a percentage of compensation. Despite what the name implies, profit-sharing
plans are not dependent on corporate profits for contributions to be
made. Contribution levels may be changed from one year to the
next. Plan participants generally do not control how the contributions are invested.

401(k) Plans

401(k) plans are defined contribution plans that are generically
known as *employee thrift and savings plans.* You, as an eligible employee, elect in advance to defer part of your compensation to the
plan, and sometimes your employer will match some or all of it.
Neither the amount deferred nor your employer-matching contribution is included in your income until distributed from the plan.

A common level of employer-matching contribution is 50 cents for
every dollar the employee contributes, up to a set percentage limit.
For example, your employer may contribute 3 percent of your compensation if you contribute 6 percent. It is like a guaranteed 50
percent first-year return on the amount you contribute each year.
Your own contributions are vested immediately, but your right to
keep the matching contributions depends on the plan's vesting
schedule. Matching contributions must vest either all at once after
no more than three years, or at a rate of 20 percent each year

starting with the second year of service. Employer matching contributions that were made before 2002 are permitted to vest at a somewhat slower rate.

Observation

As an employee eligible for matching contributions, you should make every effort to contribute at least the amount that will entitle you to the maximum available employer-matching contribution.

As a 401(k) plan participant, you generally make your own investment decisions, usually by choosing among a variety of funds selected by your employer.

401(k) Contribution Limits

For 2004, the maximum amount that you can elect to defer to a 401(k) plan is $13,000, subject to certain overall limits. Future contribution limits will increase considerably, as shown in the chart on page 80. If you are over 50 by the end of a year, you will be allowed to make even larger contributions. Also, contributions you can make up to the dollar maximums are no longer limited by any set percentage of your compensation.

Observation

This means that you may contribute the maximum dollar amount to your 401(k) plan for a year, even if that amount is half, three-quarters, or even all of your salary for the year. This important change will be especially useful in boosting retirement savings of a second family earner with modest earnings. Under previous law, the amount these lower-paid individuals could contribute was very small.

Caution

Although the law now allows 401(k) deferrals of up to 100 percent of pay, this option will be available only in plans that are amended to eliminate any lower percentage of compensation limits previously specified in the plan.

Example

Sarah, who is 47 years old, reenters the workforce in 2004 on a part-time basis after a child care hiatus of 15 years. Her employer maintains a 401(k) plan in which Sarah is eligible to participate after three months of service. Sarah's husband earns enough to support the family, and Sarah wants to put as much of her earnings as possible into a retirement plan on a pretax basis. Sarah expects to earn $10,000 in compensation in 2004 during the time she is eligible to make elective 401(k) deferrals. Result: If Sarah wishes to, she may contribute 100 percent of compensation to the plan. Only the annual dollar limit on 401(k) contributions (and her FICA tax liability) would reduce the amount she can contribute.

Annual 401(k) Elective Deferral Limits*

Year	Under Age 50 ($)	Age 50 or Older ($) (Includes Catch-Up)
2004	13,000	16,000
2005	14,000	18,000
2006 and later	15,000 as indexed	20,000 as indexed

* Not more than 100 percent of compensation.

Note that even though these pretax contributions allow you to avoid immediate income tax, they are subject to Social Security tax (if you are below the FICA wage base) and Medicare tax.

Special nondiscrimination rules apply to 401(k) elective deferrals, but those rules won't limit the catch-up contributions you make if you are age 50 or over. If your employer chooses to match catch-up contributions, the matching contributions will be subject to the usual nondiscrimination rules that apply to other employer-matching contributions.

Observation

The reductions to the tax rates for capital gains and dividends (discussed in Chapters 1 and 2) should have little impact on the decision whether to participate in 401(k) plans. The combination of tax deductions, tax-deferred accumulation, and the potential for employer-matching contributions should continue to make these plans the first choice savings vehicle for retirement (despite the fact that distributions are subject to ordinary tax rates). There also is a psychological benefit associated with payroll deductions that makes it painless and easy to invest. Further, access to the funds prior to retirement is restricted, thus reducing the temptation to spend.

The only taxpayers who should reconsider participation are older taxpayers who are close to retirement, receive no company match, and expect to be in a higher tax bracket later.

For Small Employers

The savings incentive match plan for employees (SIMPLE) can be set up by companies with 100 or fewer employees that don't offer other types of retirement plans. As its name implies, a SIMPLE plan is easier and less expensive to set up and administer than a standard qualified retirement plan. Under this type of plan, employees may defer up to $9,000 for 2004. (For later years, see the chart on page 82.) Employers that offer a SIMPLE generally must make a nonelective or matching contribution in the 2 to 3 percent range on behalf of each plan participant.

The contribution limits on deferrals by employees to SIMPLE plans are shown in the following table:

SIMPLE Plan Maximum Deferrals*

Year	Under Age 50 ($)	Age 50 or Older ($) (Includes Catch-Up)
2004	9,000	10,500
2005	10,000	12,000
2006 and later	10,000 as indexed	12,500 as indexed

* Not more than 100 percent of compensation.

Defined Benefit Pension Plans

Unlike a defined contribution plan, a defined benefit plan—commonly called a pension plan—pays a fixed monthly amount of income at retirement. The benefit is determined using a formula specified in the plan, usually based on your salary and the number of years you have worked for your employer. Some companies increase pension benefits during retirement to help overcome the impact of inflation.

You are entitled to your monthly pension benefit whether or not the plan contributions have been invested well. If the value of the investments falls below the amount needed to fund the promised benefit, the employer must contribute more to the plan, so you do not bear the risk of bad investments or a severe market downturn. If the plan ceases to exist, the Pension Benefit Guaranty Corporation (PBGC) pays promised benefits up to a certain level. Defined benefit plans generally do not require or allow employee contributions.

If you retire early, you will usually receive a reduced benefit and if you work beyond normal retirement age, you receive an increased amount when you begin to collect benefits as indexed.

Increase in Benefit Limit

The maximum annual benefit that a defined benefit pension plan can fund in 2004 is $170,000. This amount will be indexed for future inflation. The limit is somewhat lower for benefits beginning before age 62 and higher for payments beginning after age 65.

Nonqualified Deferred Compensation Plans

Nonqualified plans are used to reward individual executives, or other employees, without the need to treat all individuals similarly—if a company is willing to forgo current tax deductions for its contributions. (The company's deduction is delayed until the year the income is taxed to the executive.)

> ### *Observation*
>
> If you are a highly compensated employee, consider the benefits of coverage under a nonqualified plan. These plans offer the benefits of tax deferral on both the principal and income, as well as the ability to set aside larger amounts of retirement assets than do most qualified plans.

> ### *Caution*
>
> The employee is treated as a general creditor of the employer in the event that the company enters bankruptcy. This means that if your employer goes bankrupt, you have to get in line with all the other general creditors to get a portion of your employer's remaining assets, and you may lose all of your nonqualified plan benefits.

Under a deferred compensation plan, you elect to defer a portion of your salary or bonus until a future date (for example, retirement). To get the tax savings, you generally must agree to defer the compensation before the period in which it is earned or awarded.

Your Resources

Planning for retirement can include making contributions to Keogh plans, other self-employed retirement plans such as SEPs, or IRAs, and making after-tax contributions to employer plans and 401(k) plans if they are available to you. Make sure you maximize the tax benefits by carefully considering the type of plan and whether contributions are deductible.

Observation

For most people, deductible individual retirement accounts (IRAs), simplified employee pensions (SEPs), and Keoghs should not be impacted by reduced tax rates on capital gains and dividends discussed in Chapters 1 and 2. The immediate tax deduction combined with tax-deferred growth continues to provide an attractive after-tax potential (despite the ordinary income tax treatment on distributions). These accounts are particularly attractive for portfolios that produce significant short-term capital gains or ordinary income.

Caution

The benefits of deductible retirement savings are not as certain for taxpayers:

- Over age 70½ (only Keogh and SEP contributions are allowed for these people, but not IRA contributions).
- With an asset allocation heavy on dividend paying stocks and low portfolio turnover.
- Who expect to be in a higher tax bracket during payout.

Keogh Plans

If you are self-employed, you can maximize your retirement savings by taking advantage of self-employed retirement fund (Keogh plan) contributions. You can make a deductible contribution to your own retirement plan for a year up to the due date (including extensions) of your return. But the plan itself must be set up by the end of the year for which the contribution is made to take advantage of this deferred payment rule.

There are three general types of Keogh plans from which to choose:

1. **Profit-sharing plan.** Annual contributions may be discretionary, up to a certain percentage of self-employment income.

2. **Money purchase plan.** Yearly contributions based on a chosen percentage of self-employment income are mandatory.

Observation

The increased profit-sharing contribution and deduction limits generally eliminate the need to have a money purchase plan. Previously, a profit-sharing plan was often set up in tandem with a money purchase plan to provide the then-maximum deduction of 25 percent of compensation while giving the employer some flexibility to alter contribution percentages if needed. Now that the deduction limit for regular profit-sharing plans has been raised to 25 percent, however, the mandatory contribution required by a money purchase plan can be eliminated without giving up the ability to make 25 percent deductible contributions.

3. **Defined benefit plan.** Contributions are based on complex calculations. Although this is the most expensive kind of plan to operate, older, highly compensated, self-employed individuals usually find that it permits them to make the largest tax deductible contributions.

Keogh contribution and deduction limits are the same as those for other qualified retirement plans, with adjustments for the way the self-employed's earned income is calculated.

Observation

If you are self-employed and have employees, you must remember that Keogh plans are subject to complex nondiscrimination and coverage rules. You generally can't cover just yourself if you have half-time or full-time employees over the age of 21 who have worked for you for a year or more.

Simplified Employee Pension Plans

If you are self-employed or have a small company, you can also choose to use this IRA-type plan in which a percentage of net self-employment income is contributed to the plan (similar to a defined contribution Keogh plan). Unlike Keogh plans, SEPs can be established as late as the extended tax return due date for the prior tax year. SEPs must also provide comparable benefits for employees who satisfy certain liberal eligibility requirements. Recent law changes made SEPs much more attractive by eliminating their lower 15 percent maximum contribution and replacing it with a 25 percent contribution limit to match that of other defined contribution plans. While simpler to administer than regular Keogh plans, SEPs provide fewer options than Keogh plans do for accumulating large retirement benefits, especially for older plan participants. New SEPs also cannot offer 401(k) features, such as income deferral by employees.

Traditional and Roth IRAs

Any person under age $70\frac{1}{2}$ (or older for Roth IRAs) with at least $3,000 of earned income during 2004 can establish an IRA and contribute the maximum amount to it. There are two very different types of IRAs (more detail concerning each type follows):

1. **Traditional IRAs.** Contributions are deductible if the IRA owner is not covered by a qualified retirement plan or if income limits are not exceeded; distributions are fully or partly taxable. Those whose income level is too high to take deductions for these contributions may make nondeductible contributions. Distributions from traditional IRAs are taxable when received and are subject to a 10 percent excise tax if taken before age 59½ (with certain limited exceptions).

2. **Roth IRAs.** While contributions are not deductible, earnings paid to you from these accounts are tax-free as long as certain requirements are met. Generally, the account must exist for at least five tax years, and you must receive the funds after you've reached age 59½, or as a result of death or disability. If you meet the income requirements to make Roth IRA contributions, you should seriously consider doing so. Roth IRAs are an excellent retirement vehicle.

The maximum amount that you can contribute to a Roth IRA for a year phases out over an AGI range of $95,000 to $110,000 for singles and $150,000 to $160,000 for married joint-return filers. If you are not above these income levels, you may make a contribution even if you participate in an employer-sponsored retirement plan. If your income is above these levels, you are ineligible to contribute to a Roth IRA.

Observation

Contributing to a Roth IRA is still advantageous relative to taxable investments, even after the reductions in capital gains and dividends tax rates. Roth IRAs generate tax-free income and aren't subject to the required lifetime distribution rules that govern other IRAs.

Higher Contribution Limits

The maximum annual IRA contribution limit and catch-up contributions for those 50 or older as of the end of a year will increase, as shown in the following table. The higher limit applies to both traditional and Roth IRAs:

Increased IRA Contribution Limits

Year	Regular ($)	Catch-Up ($)
2004	3,000	500
2005	4,000	500
2006	4,000	1,000
2007	4,000	1,000
2008 and later	5,000	1,000

Observation

The increase in maximum IRA contributions gives you greater opportunities to save for retirement on a tax-favored basis and will help you to rely less on employer retirement plans and Social Security.

Observation

The income limits have not changed for contributions to deductible IRAs by those who are active participants in qualified plans; eligibility to contribute to a Roth IRA, or conversion of a traditional IRA to a Roth IRA have. If you are a high income taxpayer, you can make modestly larger contributions to nondeductible regular IRAs.

Observation

It makes less sense to make nondeductible contributions to a traditional IRA now that capital gains and dividend income are taxed at a maximum rate of only 15 percent, or 5 percent for those in the two lowest tax brackets, except perhaps for the fact that these rates currently are not permanent. Because capital gains and dividends that are earned within an IRA are taxed at ordinary income rates when distributed, they lose the benefit of the preferential rates. Also, funds in the IRA are subject to required distribution beginning at age $70\frac{1}{2}$, as described later in this chapter, whereas investments outside of the IRA don't have to be liquidated at any set time.

There has always been a school of thought that only long-term periods of deferral would justify the use of nondeductible IRAs (since they can convert lower tax-rate income into higher tax rate income). The reduced tax rates on dividends and long-term capital gains only add fuel to the debate. For portfolios that produce significant short-term capital gains or ordinary income, nondeductible IRAs may remain attractive, especially for those far from payout status. Also, younger taxpayers should continue to consider nondeductible IRAs, since long periods of tax deferral may overcome the other disadvantages associated with them.

One other point to consider is the implication of sunset of the lower dividend and capital gains rates in 2009 and the potential for lost IRA opportunity. If these rates are not made permanent, taxpayers who passed on nondeductible IRAs for several years will not be able to make up those contributions.

Traditional IRAs

Your ability to make tax-deductible contributions to a traditional IRA is limited by your income level if you are an active participant in your employer-sponsored retirement plan. The maximum deductible contribution you can make phases out over the following income levels (see Table 3.1).

Table 3.1 Phase-Out of IRA Deductions for Employer Plan Participants				
	Singles and Heads of Households Deduction ($)		Married Filing Joint Returns Deduction ($)	
Year	Full	No	Full	No
2004	45,000	55,000	65,000	75,000
2005	50,000	60,000	70,000	80,000
2006	50,000	60,000	75,000	85,000
2007 and later	50,000	60,000	80,000	100,000

If you are married, but you and your spouse file separately, your deduction phase-out range is from zero to $10,000 of adjusted gross income (AGI), effectively preventing each of you from taking IRA deductions in almost all cases in which at least one spouse is an active participant in an employer-sponsored retirement plan.

A nonworking spouse or a working spouse who is not a participant in a qualified retirement plan, but whose spouse is, has a greater opportunity to make tax-deductible contributions to a regular IRA on a joint return even though the working spouse is an active retirement plan participant. The availability of this deduction phases out for couples with an AGI between $150,000 and $160,000.

Observation

If you qualify, you should always make a contribution to a Roth IRA rather than making a nondeductible contribution to a traditional IRA. No deduction is allowed in either case, but the earnings on nondeductible traditional IRA contributions will be taxed to you at ordinary income rates when you take distributions, whereas there is the potential for completely tax-free distributions from the Roth IRA. Also, there is no requirement that amounts in Roth IRAs be distributed to you during your lifetime, as there is with traditional IRAs. This allows you to keep the Roth IRA's tax shelter going for your entire life, if you so choose, and pass the tax-free earnings on to your heirs.

Conversions to Roth IRAs

Preexisting IRAs may be converted into Roth IRAs if your income is less than $100,000 (regardless of whether you are single or married). You'll have to pay income tax on these conversions, but not the 10 percent penalty that applies to early IRA withdrawals. Distributions from a Roth IRA within five years of the conversion that come from converted amounts will be subject to the 10 percent penalty tax.

Observation

Consider converting a traditional IRA invested in equities or stock mutual funds to a Roth IRA when stock values are depressed. The tax cost will be based on the low valuations at the time of the conversion, and no tax will be owed on future price recoveries.

Observation

Starting in 2005, more elderly individuals may qualify to convert their traditional IRAs to Roth IRAs. Post-age 70$\frac{1}{2}$ required minimum distributions are no longer taken into account for the $100,000 income limit on conversion eligibility.

You can change your mind and undo a conversion from a traditional IRA to a Roth IRA by transferring the funds back to a regular IRA in a direct trustee-to-trustee transfer. This will eliminate the tax liability from the conversion. You might need to do this, for example, if your AGI for the conversion year exceeds the $100,000 income limit, making you ineligible to convert. Or you may want to switch back if the value of the assets in the Roth IRA has dropped, and you don't want to pay tax on the conversion based on the higher value of the assets on the conversion date. If you convert to a Roth IRA in 2004, you will have until October 15, 2005 to transfer it back to a traditional IRA, assuming you file a timely 2004 tax return, including extensions. If you file your return before undoing the conversion, you'll need to file an amended return to report the reversal and eliminate your tax liability from the conversion.

If you have switched back to a regular IRA from a Roth IRA, you can reconvert to another Roth IRA and have your tax liability figured on the basis of the later conversion. However, you cannot reconvert until the start of the year after the original Roth IRA conversion was made, or, if later, more than 30 days after you switched the Roth IRA back to a traditional IRA.

Example

John converted a $100,000 IRA brokerage account (to which he had made only deductible contributions) to a Roth IRA in January 2004, giving him $100,000 of taxable income on the conversion. If the value of that Roth IRA account fell to $70,000 in July 2004, John would nonetheless be liable for tax on $100,000. However, if he transfers the $70,000 directly back to a traditional IRA, he will wipe out his tax liability from the conversion. Then he can re-convert to another Roth IRA after the waiting period has passed (explained earlier), perhaps before the value of the assets in the traditional IRA has fully recovered.

Observation

When it comes to IRAs, the earlier contributions are made, the better. Take the case of a 22-year-old who contributes $2,000 annually to an IRA for just 10 years, stopping after age 31. Assuming an annual growth rate of 10 percent, the assets in that IRA will increase to approximately $895,000 by the time the IRA owner is 65 years old, even though he has contributed only $20,000 to the account.

Contrast that with a person who waits until age 32 to start con-tributing to an IRA, but contributes $2,000 for 33 years. The funds also earn 10 percent, but at age 65 this person's account balance is only about $540,000—that is $355,000 less than the IRA of the person who started contributing at age 22, despite $46,000 more in contributions.

Once you establish the retirement savings vehicle or vehicles that are in line with your goals (and, obviously, for which you are eligible and that are available to you), you should contribute early and regularly to benefit more fully from the effects of tax-free compounding.

Observation

You do not have to wait until you are sure of your income for a year to contribute to an IRA. You can give to either a regular IRA or a Roth IRA at any time and switch accounts by Octo-ber 15 of the following year (if you have extended your tax

(continued)

Continued

return due date until then). For example, if you make a Roth IRA contribution or conversion during 2004 and it turns out that your income for that year is more than the allowable limit, you can transfer the funds and their earnings to a regular IRA (deductible or nondeductible, depending on your circumstances).

Observation

Because many people in their teens and early twenties do not earn enough to save on a regular basis, this is an excellent opportunity for parents and grandparents to give their children and grandchildren a long-term gift costing a fraction of its ultimate value. If your children or grandchildren work, consider helping them set up an IRA to capitalize on the big benefits of tax-deferred compounding (tax-free compounding with a Roth IRA) over long periods of time.

It is amazing how much the investment can grow if a contribution is made to a tax-favored retirement plan early in life. For example, if you contributed $2,000 per year for your child or grandchild while she was age 16 through 22, and never contributed another dime, assuming a 10 percent growth rate, she would have a retirement fund at age 65 of about $1.2 million, with only $14,000 in total contributions.

Observation

Giving funds to a Roth IRA for a child or grandchild will also allow the child or grandchild to withdraw $10,000 of earnings tax- and penalty-free to put toward the purchase of a first home.

Tax Credit for Retirement Saving

Taxpayers with modest incomes now have another reason to save for their retirement. Through 2006, they may be eligible for a nonrefundable tax credit if they contribute to qualified retirement plans and IRAs. The maximum annual contribution eligible for the credit is $2,000 per individual. The credit is in addition to any deduction available.

For the lowest-income individuals (up to an AGI of $30,000 for joint return filers; $22,500 for heads of households; $15,000 for all others), the credit is 50 percent of the eligible contribution. That would be a $1,000 tax credit for a $2,000 contribution. The credit rate phases down from 50 percent to 10 percent of the contribution as AGI increases. It is totally phased out for those with an AGI above $50,000 for joint filers, $37,500 for heads of households, and $25,000 for singles. This credit is not available to students, taxpayers under 18, or dependents.

Observation

This credit will be available to many young taxpayers who are out of school but whose salaries are still modest. Be sure to tell your children about the new credit and encourage or help them to get started on their retirement saving.

Charitable Remainder Trusts

Another vehicle to consider for funding a portion of your retirement is a charitable remainder trust. Although complex rules apply, funding such trusts with appreciated securities can provide an alternative to traditional qualified and nonqualified plans because they allow you to improve your cash flow on a pretax basis.

Tax-Deferred Annuities

If you have made the maximum permitted 401(k) or 403(b) contribution, contributed to an IRA, and have a decent portfolio of stocks designed to take advantage of favorable capital gains rates when the stocks are ultimately sold, you may want to consider a tax-deferred annuity. The investment earnings (usually from name-brand mutual funds and other investment alternatives) can compound tax deferred within the annuity vehicle until they are withdrawn. It is important to remember that annuities will ultimately be taxed at ordinary income tax rates (not capital gains tax rates) when distributed to you, as with a traditional IRA, even if the money is invested in mutual funds that would have been taxed at a 15 percent rate if held outside the annuity. Annuities are similar to IRAs in that there is a 10 percent excise tax generally applied to withdrawals prior to age 59. Annuities offer a guaranteed payment option that will assure a fixed level of payment for your life. You should examine the expenses and fees charged by the insurance company issuing the annuity to ensure that they are competitive with other investments. You might also consider the universal variable life insurance policy alternative discussed on the next page.

Observation

Deferred annuities are less advantageous now that capital gains and dividend income are taxed at a maximum rate of only 15 percent, except perhaps for the fact that these rates currently are not permanent. Because capital gains and dividends that are earned within an annuity are taxed at ordinary income rates when distributed, they lose the benefit of the preferential rates. However, younger taxpayers should continue to consider annuities, since long periods of tax deferral may overcome their other disadvantages.

Split-Dollar Life Insurance

Split-dollar life insurance traditionally has been a popular tax advantaged way to provide life insurance protection to valued employees and company owners. Split-dollar isn't a type of insurance, but rather is a method of dividing the ownership and rights in a cash value life insurance policy among different parties—frequently an employer and an employee.

Under the most basic split-dollar arrangement, the employer pays most if not all policy premiums each year. The employee may or may not pay a portion of the premium. The employee's payment is measured by the cost of the life insurance coverage (that is, actual term cost). If the employee did not pay, then he or she recognized income from the fringe benefit.

The employer retains the right to receive the premium advancements back from the policy proceeds at death. The employee is able to name beneficiaries for the remaining amount. The employee may actually own the policy.

If the employee owns the policy, it is known as *collateral assignment* because the employer has a portion of the policy assigned to the employer as collateral for premium advancements. If the employer owns the policy, it is known as *endorsement* because the employer endorses a portion of the death benefit to employee control.

Many complex—and advantageous—split-dollar arrangements have been developed over the years. Of particular interest to the IRS are arrangements that entitle the employee to at least some of the policy's cash value. These arrangements are known as *equity* split-dollar. The IRS concluded that the split-dollar tax rules needed to change in reaction to the widespread use of equity split-dollar arrangements.

As a result, the IRS issued some highly complex rules that it hopes capture all of the economic benefits received. These new rules will *NOT* apply to arrangements in place before September 18, 2003, and not materially modified thereafter. Thus, in theory, the new rules do not apply to preexisting split-dollar arrangements. In fact, the IRS has indicated that it will apply some of the new rules to arrangements in place before September 18, 2003, that are terminated before death.

The new rules determine taxation based on who owns the policy and who pays the premiums. Endorsement arrangements will continue to be treated under historical split-dollar rules with some additional features relative to "equity" movements. For example, the nonowner of the policy will be taxed on the policy's cash value that is accessible to him. Collateral assignment arrangements will generally be treated as loans from the employer to the employee.

The new rules have also caused a reexamination of the original purpose to the arrangement as well as the policy performance. Often, goals and objectives may have changed or the policy performance may have suffered due to general market conditions. In any event, the new rules make split-dollar arrangements (especially equity arrangements) more tax costly.

Observation

These split-dollar rules are now extremely complex, and anyone with an existing split-dollar arrangement or contemplating entering into one needs to get professional advice.

Universal Variable Life Insurance

Instead of a tax-deferred annuity that will be taxed on withdrawal, think about universal variable life insurance. Like its cousin, the tax-deferred annuity, the universal variable life insurance policy has an investment component consisting of mutual funds or other investment choices. The investment earnings compound on a tax-deferred basis within the life insurance policy until they are withdrawn.

One benefit is that you can borrow the investment earnings tax-free. At death, unborrowed earnings are added to the face value of the policy and can be paid to beneficiaries on a tax-free basis. You should examine the expenses and fees charged by the insurance company issuing the policy to ensure that they are competitive with similar investments.

Long-term deferral periods are needed to make the tax-free buildup overcome the "drag" on accumulations created by mortality and administration costs associated with life insurance. Since all "loaned" amounts are received income tax free, the character of earnings within the policy is not important. Only if something goes wrong with this high-maintenance technique are income taxes triggered. When triggered, all income is subject to ordinary income tax rates (like an IRA or annuity). If something does go wrong, all the income built up in the policy is taxable at a single time (a financial disaster).

Observation

This strategy is unlikely to be undercut because of reduced rates on dividends and long-term capital gains. The strategy is to use the income tax-free nature of life insurance to build up a significant pool of assets, and then draw on that pool by "borrowing" from the policy during retirement years.

Professional Retirement Services

You and your spouse may be able to take advantage of tax-free retirement services from your employer. Your employer can provide this service as a nontaxable fringe benefit.

> ### Observation
>
> Retirement planning has become a very complicated, difficult process involving important income tax, investing, estate planning, and other family-related issues. This nontaxable fringe benefit should give you better access to professionals who can help you choose the right tools and make the right decisions when considering the complex options and opportunities now available when planning for your retirement.

Social Security

If you receive Social Security payments, you may be taxed on some of the payments you receive. Benefits must be included in income if your modified AGI (which generally includes AGI, tax-exempt interest, and certain foreign-source income with other minor adjustments) plus one-half of your Social Security benefits exceeds a certain base amount. The base amount begins at $25,000 for single individuals and $32,000 for married couples filing jointly. The amount of benefits included in taxable income is the lesser of one-half of benefits received or one-half of the excess of modified AGI plus 50 percent of benefits received over the base amount. A second threshold of $34,000 for singles and $44,000 for joint returns results in more of your benefits being taxable. If this threshold is exceeded, you must include the lesser of 85 percent of benefits or the sum of the lesser of the amount included under the old rules or $6,000 ($4,500 for singles) plus 85 percent of the amount by which modified AGI, increased by 50 percent of Social Security benefits, exceeds $44,000 ($34,000 for single individuals).

> ### Observation
>
> The calculation of taxable Social Security benefits is not a simple one. It is often loosely stated that this provision will subject 50 percent or 85 percent of Social Security benefits to tax. In many cases, determining the amount of benefits actually subject to tax involves complicated calculations.

Observation

Because the second threshold for the tax on Social Security benefits for married filers is only $10,000 more than that for single filers, a substantial "marriage penalty" results. For example, an unmarried couple filing separately, each with total income of $37,000—$12,000 of which is from Social Security—would each be taxed on $3,000 of his or her Social Security benefits. If they were married filing jointly, however, $20,400 of their Social Security benefits would be taxed.

Observation

The Social Security Administration now sends annual statements detailing an individual's earnings, contributions, and estimated future benefits. If you haven't received these benefit statements, use Form SSA-7004, Request for Earnings and Benefit Estimate Statement, to obtain a listing of your lifetime earnings and an estimate of your Social Security benefit. There is a limited period of time in which to correct mistakes.

Observation

The earnings limit, which previously reduced Social Security benefits by $1 for every $3 that benefits recipients age 65 through 69 earned over a certain limit, has been repealed (the earnings limit for those 62 through 65 is still in effect). As a result, those who work beyond their full retirement age no longer have their benefits reduced. However, earnings limits still apply before full retirement age (see page 255).

To get information about the Social Security system, see www.ssa.gov, the Social Security Administration web site.

Required Retirement Plan Distributions

You must begin to take at least a specified minimum amount of distributions from your qualified plans and traditional IRAs by April 1 of the year after the year you turn 70½. However, if you are still working at that time and you aren't at least a 5 percent owner of your company, you do not have to begin to take distributions from a company retirement plan until April 1 of the year after you retire. If you don't take the minimum distribution, you will have to pay a 50 percent excise tax. Obviously, this is something to avoid.

> ### Observation
>
> Minimum distributions are not required from Roth IRAs during the life of the owner. This allows the tax advantages of Roth IRAs to continue until the Roth IRA owner's death and allows the income tax-free benefits to be passed to a spouse or other family member.

After years of criticism, the IRS finalized and simplified these rules. The new rules are simpler, generally spread payouts over a longer time, and give you more flexibility in naming and changing beneficiaries. You now figure your required distribution simply by dividing your account balance at the end of the previous year by a factor for your age that comes from an IRS table (see Table 3.2). You use this method even if you had been using older rules in the past. You use the same factor whether or not you have named a beneficiary, and if so, no matter how old the beneficiary is. (The only exception is if you have named your spouse as your beneficiary and he or she is more than 10 years younger than you. In that case, required distributions are based on your joint life expectancy and are even lower.)

Table 3.2	*Uniform Lifetime Table for Use by Owners*		
Age	**Distribution Period**	**Age**	**Distribution Period**
70	27.4	93	9.6
71	26.5	94	9.1
72	25.6	95	8.6
73	24.7	96	8.1
74	23.8	97	7.6
75	22.9	98	7.1
76	22.0	99	6.7
77	21.2	100	6.3
78	20.3	101	5.9
79	19.5	102	5.5
80	18.7	103	5.2
81	17.9	104	4.9
82	17.1	105	4.5
83	16.3	106	4.2
84	15.5	107	3.9
85	14.8	108	3.7
86	14.1	109	3.4
87	13.4	110	3.1
88	12.7	111	2.9
89	12.0	112	2.6
90	11.4	113	2.4
91	10.8	114	2.1
92	10.2	115 and over	1.9

Required distributions now are almost always smaller than under the old rules. If you are taking distributions based on whom you named as beneficiary and whether you recalculate life expectancy, you are using the old, complex, and repealed rules.

Caution

Make sure that your required minimum IRA distribution is figured using the newest rules. For most people, the amount that must be distributed is much lower than the minimum distribution that was required under the old rules.

There also are now more workable rules for distributions after the account owner's death. If you have named a beneficiary, the remaining amounts in the account are usually distributed over the beneficiary's remaining life expectancy. If you haven't designated a beneficiary, distributions can be made over a period no longer than your remaining life expectancy at the time of death. If you hadn't started taking distributions and didn't name a beneficiary, the balance remaining in your account at death would have to be paid out within five years, which doesn't afford much of a tax advantage to your survivors. As a result, it is very important that you name beneficiaries for your accounts and keep beneficiary designations updated as circumstances change.

Through postdeath planning, such as use of disclaimers, the postdeath distribution deferral can be maximized (that is, "stretched out"). Note that postdeath estate or trust distributions cannot be used to "stretch out" distributions. If your surviving spouse is the sole beneficiary of your IRA, he or she is allowed to treat it as his or her own and name new beneficiaries, which can further extend the tax-deferral. However, that's generally not the case if the IRA is held in trust for your spouse.

Observation

Beneficiary designation planning can provide children or grand-children with substantial funds for tax-deferred compounding during their lifetimes. It is generally not advisable to name as the beneficiary either trusts that are not carefully structured to receive distributions or your estate.

Observation

If you continue to work past age $70\frac{1}{2}$, you can hold off taking distributions from employer retirement accounts, but not from regular IRAs, until your actual retirement date, as long as you are not a 5 percent owner of the business for which the plan was established.

Observation

Roth IRAs are exempt from the rules requiring distributions to begin at age $70\frac{1}{2}$. Tax-free buildup can continue within a Roth IRA for your entire life. If you don't need the money during your lifetime, this can increase the amount of income tax-free accumulations in the account to pass to children and grandchildren.

Observation

Some participants in qualified retirement plans may receive favorable tax treatment if they receive a lump-sum distribution that is not rolled over to another qualified plan or IRA. Employees who receive appreciated securities of the employer as part of the lump-sum distribution from a qualified plan pay regular

(continued)

Continued

income tax only on the original cost of the stock (to the plan trustee). Tax on the value of the stock is at capital gains rates only when the stock is sold (capital gains from the original cost to the selling price). This special exception is known as net unrealized appreciation on employer securities. Further, employees born before 1936 may be eligible for capital gains treatment on any portion of the lump-sum that represents accumulations before 1974. The 2003 Tax Act's lower capital gains rate may encourage eligible employees to take advantage of these options.

The tax law makes it easier than ever for Americans to be financially secure in their later years by saving in retirement plans and IRAs. Whether all taxpayers are financially able as well as willing to make the change is another matter. This book is an effort to smooth the learning curve for everybody.

These retirement planning suggestions and techniques are not universally applicable; each person must pick and choose among them depending on individual circumstances. The government is providing more tax help for retirement saving, and the tax breaks stretch across the income spectrum.

We turn next to the effects of recent tax changes on home ownership. Most people do not give much thought to the federal tax implications of owning a home. They know they can deduct mortgage interest and real estate taxes, but, in fact, many other aspects of owning a home have tax consequences.

Idea Checklist

☑   Maximize participation in employer plans, especially if your employer "matches" 401(k) plan contributions. Consider contributing the maximum amount permitted.

☑ If you are 50 or older, consider making extra catch-up contributions.

☑ Make your IRA contributions at the beginning of each calendar year to maximize the tax-deferred build up.

☑ Self-employed individuals should consider which self-employment retirement plan is best for them. Remember that Keogh plans need to be established before year-end for a tax deduction, although actual contributions can be made as late as the extended tax return due date.

☑ Consider reallocating investments between tax-deferred and taxable accounts to maximize tax breaks for capital gains and dividends.

☑ Contribute to a Roth IRA if your income level permits. This may be done even if you are in a qualified retirement plan and are not permitted to make deductible contributions to a traditional IRA. A Roth IRA is especially desirable if you want to avoid making lifetime distributions required by traditional IRAs. Traditional IRAs have detailed distribution requirements.

☑ Consider whether converting a preexisting IRA to a Roth IRA makes sense for you and whether you can manage the tax liability generated from the conversion. This can be an especially good move when stock prices are depressed.

☑ Fund a Roth or other IRA for children and grandchildren who have earnings but insufficient cash flow to contribute to their own retirement plans.

☑ A charitable remainder trust can improve retirement cash flow if funded with highly appreciated assets.

☑ Review your beneficiary designations on retirement accounts to maximize the family's income-deferral opportunities.

Chapter 4

TAX ADVANTAGES OF HOME OWNERSHIP

Home ownership carries with it many special tax advantages. This chapter takes up the tax considerations of home ownership in detail and explains how to use the Tax Code provisions to minimize federal tax bills. For instance, a home office has become easier to claim as a deduction. There are tax advantages for vacation home rentals, but the rules on how to treat rental fees and expenses need careful study. Interest on limited amounts of home-equity loans is fully deductible for ordinary income tax calculations, however the proceeds are used. But when calculating the alternative minimum tax (AMT), if the loan proceeds are not used for investment purposes, you can deduct home-equity loan interest only to the extent that the loan was used to improve the house. "Points" paid to secure mortgages from a bank or other lender may be treated in several ways. Finally, there are special tax breaks on gains incurred when selling a house.

The 2001 Tax Act will have some interesting effects on homeowners' finances as the changes are phased in over the next decade. The 2003 Tax Act's rate cuts and capital gains reductions also will have an impact.

For instance, some married taxpayers whose itemized deductions are small may stop itemizing deductions now that the standard deduction for married couples has increased to twice that for singles. This increase in the standard deduction, however, lasts only through 2004, after which it drops back a bit and then gradually climbs once more until it again is double the standard deduction amount for singles in 2009. For some taxpayers, this increased standard deduction exceeds the total deductions that they could claim by itemizing. Homeowners will not complain if this happens since their total taxes will decline and their tax situation will be simplified. Some may choose to sell their homes and rent, using the freed capital for other investments. Those who already rent out their homes will benefit from the new lower tax rates on their rental income.

Homeowners who continue to itemize will find their deductions worth slightly less than before because tax rates are lower. This will be particularly true for those who benefit by dropping out of the 25 percent bracket now that the upper limit of the 15 percent bracket has been raised for married couples to twice the size of the 15 percent bracket for singles.

The biggest tax law change regarding home ownership for wealthier individuals is that capital gains taxes are now lower on the profit on the sale of a principal residence that exceeds the amount that is tax-free. Before May 6, 2003, the tax on the gain in excess of $250,000 ($500,000 for married couples) was 20 percent. Now it is only 15 percent.

Techniques and tools that will help you maximize the tax benefits of owning a home are discussed in this chapter.

Tax Benefits of Owning a Home

Generally, you can deduct interest that is paid during the tax year on several types of debt related to your home or on home-equity loans, as long as they are secured by a qualified residence (your principal residence and one other home).

Mortgage Interest

You can deduct interest on debt incurred in acquiring, constructing, or substantially improving a qualified residence. Together, these debts are referred to as "acquisition indebtedness." The combined amount of debt that can be considered acquisition indebtedness is capped at $1 million.

> **Observation**
>
> Debt on a maximum of two residences can be counted toward the $1 million limit. Thus, if you have a city home, a beach home, and a mountain home, only debt related to your principal residence and one of the other residences can qualify as home acquisition indebtedness.

> **Observation**
>
> If you are thinking about the purchase of a second home and you already have $1 million of acquisition indebtedness, or are thinking about purchasing a third home, consider using a trust to purchase the property, with your children as trust beneficiaries. The trust can rent the property to you at fair market value rates. In other words, if you've hit the limit either on your first home or on your first and second homes in aggregate, and you're looking to purchase another home, the trust option is a good one from a tax perspective.
>
> Margin interest cannot qualify as mortgage interest even where you borrow from your brokerage account to purchase a residence, because margin debt is secured by the assets in your account, not by the purchased home.

Home-Equity Loans

Interest is deductible on up to $100,000 of home-equity loans. For the interest to be deductible, the home-equity loan cannot exceed the fair market value of the residence, reduced by any acquisition indebtedness.

Interest paid on a home equity loan is deductible in almost all situations no matter how the loan proceeds are used. For example, the fact that home-equity loan proceeds are used to finance personal consumption, such as the purchase of a new car or paying college expenses, does not affect interest deductibility.

Observation

Consider refinancing nondeductible personal expenditures, such as an auto loan or credit card debt, with a home-equity loan. If the tax savings from the interest deduction are used to further pay down the principal portion of the loan, the debt will be paid off sooner.

Caution

Keep in mind that home-equity interest expense is not always deductible. If the debt proceeds are used to purchase municipal bonds, for example, the interest expense is not deductible.

Vacation Homes

If your vacation home is a "residence," the mortgage interest you pay is generally deductible. If your vacation home is partly your residence and partly a rental property (see the discussion that follows), your interest deduction must be prorated, along with your other expenses.

A vacation home is generally considered a residence if you use it for personal purposes for more than the greater of 14 days per year or 10 percent of the number of days the home is rented out at a fair rental value. Personal use is use by you or a co-owner of the property, or a family member of either, and use by other people who do not pay a fair market rental. Days when you are performing maintenance and repairs on a vacation property are not considered personal-use days. If you own a vacation home and rent it out to others, the amount of rental activity will affect the tax treatment of rental income:

- **More than 14 days personal use/rented fewer than 15 days.** If you rent out a home for 14 days per year or less, it qualifies as a second residence. Any rental income is tax-free, and any rental expenses are not deductible (except mortgage interest and real estate taxes).

- **More than 14 days personal use/rented more than 14 days.** If you rent out your vacation home for more than 14 days per year and your personal use *exceeds* the greater of 14 days or 10 percent of the rental period, the home is a personal residence subject to the vacation home rules. You can deduct a proportionate share of property taxes and interest attributable to your personal use. The balance of the interest and taxes can reduce the rental income. In addition, you can deduct depreciation and other operating expenses attributable to the rental to the extent of any remaining rental income. Note that you cannot claim expenses *in excess* of the rental income.

- **Fewer than 15 days personal use/rented more than 14 days.** If you rent your home for more than 14 days and your personal use *does not exceed* the greater of 14 days or 10 percent of the rental period, the vacation home is considered a rental property. Interest and taxes are allocated between personal and rental use of the property. In addition, other expenses allocable to the rental activity can be considered in full, even if this results in a loss. The loss, however, will be subject to the passive activity rules discussed next (also see Chapter 2) and generally will be deductible only to the extent of passive activity income. Interest allocated to your personal use of the home is personal interest and may not be deductible because the home generally is not considered a residence.

Rental Properties

If your vacation home is fully rented without any personal use, it is considered a rental property and is not subject to the special vacation home rules. As a rental property, taxes, interest, and other expenses are deductible, subject to the passive activity loss rules. Up to $25,000 of passive rental real estate losses can be deducted each year against other income, such as compensation and interest, if the owner meets certain "active participation" requirements.

However, the $25,000 exception is decreased for homeowners with an AGI over $100,000 and is fully phased-out for homeowners with an AGI over $150,000. Passive activity losses that can't be used currently are carried forward and can be deducted against future passive activity income, or are deducted in full when the activity that generated the losses is disposed of.

Home Office Deduction

Home is where the office is for a growing number of consultants, entrepreneurs, and telecommuters. Although expenses associated with use of a residence are generally not deductible, a home office deduction is permitted for certain expenses if a portion of the home is used exclusively and on a regular basis as the principal place of business or as a place to meet or deal with customers or clients in the ordinary course of the homeowner's trade or business.

In addition, home office deductions are available to homeowners who use a separate structure that is nearby, but not attached to the home, regularly and exclusively in connection with their trade or business.

Exclusive and Regular Use

To meet the exclusive-use requirement, you as the homeowner must use a portion of the residence solely for conducting business. There is no provision for *de minimis* personal use, such as typing a personal letter or making a personal phone call. If you are employed by a company, your use of the home office also must be "for the convenience of the employer." Generally, if your employer supplies you with an office, your home office use wouldn't meet this test.

Principal Place of Business

Until a few years ago, "principal place of business" was defined very restrictively for purposes of the home office deduction, preventing many who worked from their homes from claiming deductions.

However, a tax law change that went into effect in 1999 opened up the deduction to many more home office users. In addition to the place where the central functions of a business are performed, the term "principal place of business" now includes areas used for a business' administrative or management activities, if there is no other fixed location where the homeowner conducts these activities. This is the case even if most of the other work of the business is done outside of the home office. So, for example, it will be easier for salespeople, tradespeople, and manufacturers' representatives who work out of their homes, but perform much of their work at their customers' locations, to claim home office deductions. Here again, if you are an employee, use of your home must be for your employer's convenience to claim a home office deduction.

More people who work at home are able to take a home office deduction. Typical expenses include a portion of rent, depreciation, repairs, and utilities.

> **Observation**
>
> Under this liberalized definition of principal place of business, more individuals also are able to deduct the cost of traveling to and from their home (as their principal place of business) to other business locations. In the past, these transportation costs were considered nondeductible commuting expenses.

> **Observation**
>
> The rules about the home office deductions are still complex. A separate tax form is required with Form 1040 to claim the deduction. (Self-employed individuals claim home office expenses on Form 8829 and on Schedule C; employees use Form 2106 or Form 2106EZ and claim them as miscellaneous itemized deductions on Schedule A, Form 1040, subject to 2 percent of the AGI floor.)

Another consideration in evaluating whether it makes sense to take the deductions is that the portion of the home for which home office deductions are claimed may not qualify for the home sale exclusion described later in this chapter.

Personal Residence Trust

A first or second home is an ideal asset to transfer to a personal residence trust—a popular gift tax planning technique (see page 168). In this case, the property is transferred to the trust for a period of years, during which you retain the right to live in or use the property. At the end of the term, the property passes to whomever you choose, either in further trust or outright. The value of the transfer is discounted for gift tax purposes because of your retained right to live in the residence. In addition, all future appreciation in the value of the home is transferred free of gift tax.

Although your beneficiaries will own the residence (either in trust or outright) at the end of the trust term, you can lease the property from them at a fair rental value. If you die before the end of the trust term, the property remains in your estate. Consequently, the retained right to live in the property or to use it should be for a reasonable period given your age and general health.

> ### *Observation*
> The personal residence trust's governing instrument (the document that creates and "rules" the trust) must prohibit the trust from selling or transferring the residence, directly or indirectly, to you, your spouse, or an entity controlled by you or your spouse, during the time in which the trust is a grantor trust (a trust in which the grantor keeps some interests and control and therefore is taxed on any income from the trust). This means that the grantors will not be able to get the basis step-up at death if they live beyond the trust term. This makes a personal residence trust less attractive for homes that are already highly appreciated.

Home Sales

Principal Residence Gains Exclusion

As a home seller, you may exclude up to $250,000 of gain from the sale of your home as long as it is owned and used by you as your principal residence for at least two of the five years before the sale. Qualifying married taxpayers filing jointly may exclude up to $500,000. The full exclusion is not available if, within the two-year period before the sale, you sold another home for which you claimed the exclusion.

Qualifying for the $500,000 Exclusion

A married couple filing jointly may exclude up to $500,000 of gain from the sale of their home if:

- Either spouse owned the home for at least two of the five years preceding the sale.
- Both spouses used the home for at least two of the five years preceding the sale.
- Neither spouse sold another home at a gain within the previous two years and excluded all or part of that gain using the exclusion.

Those in the military on official extended duty (stationed at least 50 miles from home or required to live in government quarters) may elect to suspend the five-year period for up to 10 years.

Partial Exclusion

A partial exclusion may be available if you do not meet the two-year ownership and use requirement, or sell your home within two years of a previous home sale for which you used the exclusion. If you fail to meet either requirement because of a change in employment, health, or certain other unforeseen circumstances as determined by the IRS, including separation or divorce and multiple births arising from the same pregnancy, the exclusion is based on the ratio of qualifying months to 24 months (or, if less, on the ratio of the number of months between the sale date of a previous home for which the exclusion was claimed and the sale date of the current home to 24 months).

For example, suppose a single person owned and used a home as a principal residence for one year (and did not previously use the exclusion on another home sale within the previous two years) and must move for job-related reasons. The partial exclusion rule allows this person to exclude up to $125,000 of his or her gain from the sale of the residence ($250,000 exclusion times 12 divided by 24).

Partial Exclusion Rule for Joint Filers

If a married couple filing jointly doesn't meet all the conditions for claiming an exclusion of up to $500,000, the gain that is excluded on the home sale is the sum of the exclusion each spouse would be entitled to if both were single. For this purpose, each spouse is treated as owning the home for the period that either spouse owned the home.

For example, a couple sells a home that one spouse owned and used as a principal residence for 10 years and the other spouse used as a principal residence for only one year. They sell the home because of illness. They may exclude up to $375,000 of profit from the sale ($250,000 for one spouse, plus $125,000 for the other spouse).

> *Observation*
>
> Special care and planning is needed to preserve the full home sale exclusion in divorce situations.

> *Observation*
>
> Home sellers in hot, upscale real estate markets will have to pay capital gains tax on any profit above the $250,000/$500,000 limits. The rollover break that used to defer unlimited amounts of home sale gain, provided an equally expensive residence was purchased as a replacement, is no longer available. However, the 2003 Tax Act's reduced capital gains rates drop the tax on these gains from 20 percent to 15 percent for home sales after May 5, 2003. Since the new exclusion is available once every two years regardless of whether it has been used before, some homeowners may decide to sell before their gains exceed the limits. Then additional gain on their replacement residence could also qualify for the exclusion in another two years.

Observation

Because a vacation home is not your principal residence, it does not qualify for tax-free treatment when it is sold. A residence that you also use as a vacation home cannot be swapped tax-free for another property in a like-kind exchange.

Observation

However, a vacation home could become your principal residence, and, therefore, qualify for the home sale exclusion. For example, if you own a principal residence where you have resided for two or more years and a vacation home, you can sell your principal residence and get the benefit of the home sale exclusion. Then, if you move into your vacation home and establish it as your principal residence for at least two years, you can get the home sale exclusion on its sale.

Home Purchases

Real Estate Taxes

In general, real estate taxes can be deducted. In the year of a home sale, however, the Tax Code requires the deduction for real estate taxes to be apportioned between the buyer and seller according to the number of days each held the property during the year. It does not matter that your sales contract contains a different division of responsibility for the taxes.

Observation

Even though the buyer or seller might pay the entire tax, the deduction is limited by the statutory formula.

Observation

You will need your closing statement from a home sale or purchase to calculate the amount of deductible real estate taxes. You will also need to know whether the states in which you purchased or sold a home require prepayment of real estate taxes or whether such taxes are paid in arrears.

Mortgage Points

Mortgage points incurred with a home loan can be significant. A *point* is a charge paid by a borrower for taking out a loan. Each point is 1 percent of the loan amount. You must amortize most points over the life of the loan; however, you can deduct points you pay for acquiring or making improvements to your main residence in the year the debts are paid. The deductibility of points depends on whether the lender assesses them as additional interest or as a service charge. This is sometimes a difficult determination. Points are generally considered additional interest if the lender is charging for the use of money. If points are assessed for application preparation or processing, they are treated as a service charge and added to the purchaser's basis in the residence and thus are nondeductible.

Observation

Do not assume you should pay points when purchasing a new home. Think about how long you are likely to own the property. If you expect to sell the property within five years or less, it may be more advantageous to pay a slightly higher interest rate to get a no-points or low-points mortgage loan.

Points may be deducted in full during the year they were paid if the following requirements are met:

- Points are paid directly to the lender by the borrower; points are treated as paid directly to the lender if the borrower provides unborrowed funds at least equal to the points charged at the closing or as a down payment or escrow deposit.

- The loan is incurred for the purchase or improvement of a principal residence.
- Points are an established business practice in the area in which the loan originates. In other words, banks and other lending institutions in that geographical area typically impose points when granting mortgage loans.
- The dollar amount of the points is typical for the area in which the loan originates.
- The points are clearly designated as such on the settlement form.
- The points are expressed as a percentage of the loan amount.

Thus, points paid on most mortgage loans financing the purchase of principal residences are deductible. However, borrowers who do not satisfy these requirements must amortize the points over the life of the loan.

Observation

The most common situations in which points must be amortized include the purchase of a second residence and refinancing the principal home's mortgage.

Observation

The unamortized points remaining when an underlying mortgage is paid off after a sale or refinancing are deductible in full. But points on a satisfied mortgage cannot be deducted immediately on a refinancing if the same mortgage lender holds both mortgages.

Owning a home is a cornerstone of the American Dream, and a home has usually been most taxpayers' most valuable asset, both financially and emotionally. The tax law gives home ownership numerous opportunities that this chapter has described.

The next chapter discusses saving for education—a high priority under the 2001 Tax Act. In the past, many of the Tax Code's incentives for education savings were not available to taxpayers in the higher brackets. Now, however, families with relatively high incomes may be able to put away more after-tax money and withdraw the gains tax-free, which increases their flexibility for funding education for children and grandchildren. Chapter 5 looks at that in detail.

Idea Checklist

- ☑ Convert nondeductible interest expense into tax-deductible home-equity interest expense.

- ☑ Know the vacation home rules before renting out your second home.

- ☑ Consider placing a principal residence or second home in a personal residence trust.

- ☑ Review closing documents from real estate sales or purchases to find deductible real estate tax amounts.

- ☑ If you refinance your home during 2004, any remaining unamortized points on the paid-off loan are generally deductible on your 2004 return.

- ☑ Rather than paying tax on a large gain on a vacation home, consider converting it to your principal residence for two years before the sale in order to make up to $250,000/$500,000 of your gain tax-free.

Chapter 5

HOW TO MAXIMIZE SAVINGS FOR EDUCATION

To pay for a child's quality education, parents will do just about anything, even spend their life savings, assume second mortgages, and work at multiple jobs if that's what's necessary. It gets harder and harder to keep up with college tuition, which is growing far faster than the inflation rate.

Fortunately, the Tax Code now offers some real incentives to help parents fund their children's education. This chapter describes a number of helpful tuition-financing techniques. Despite the fact that there are more available tax breaks, the best advice is to put aside as much as you can as early as you can.

Until now, many of the education tax incentives weren't available to those with higher incomes. But families with higher incomes now can take advantage of some tax breaks, including what is by far the best educational tax break, the much-improved Section 529 plan. Also, many of the restrictions that previously prevented taxpayers from bundling various education tax breaks together in the same year have been eliminated.

Observation

Parents should consider the impact that Section 529 programs and Coverdell Education Savings Accounts (formerly called Education IRAs) will have on their chances of obtaining financial aid for college. Some advisors suggest that families who wish to maximize their financial aid use the types of investments that are favored in the federal financial aid formulas. These investments include retirement savings, life insurance, and home equity. However, there are many reasons not to engage in this type of planning:

- The financial aid rules may change before your child is in college.

- The favored assets under the federal formula may not be favored for your child's university-provided financial aid.

- Most financial aid is in the form of loans, not grants—why burden yourself or your child with debt?

- Only a small percentage of parental assets are applied to reduce each year's financial aid.

Qualified Section 529 Tuition Programs

For a number of years, the Tax Code has allowed states to set up "qualified state tuition programs," often referred to as Section 529 plans after the part of the Tax Code that authorizes them. States are permitted to offer two types of plans:

1. **Prepaid tuition plans** that allow a parent, grandparent, or other person to prepay tuition costs and certain other education expenses. Participants are generally allowed to put aside future tuition by contributing money to these plans, thus assuring tuition at today's tuition rate. These types of plans are generally available only to state residents and are meant to be

used for tuition at in-state public schools. About 20 states have these plans for their residents. Programs differ from state to state, however, and you have to look carefully at the details of your own state's plan.

2. **Tuition savings plans** that offer more flexibility on contribution limits and investment choices are not limited to use for attendance at in-state schools. They can be used to pay tuition, room and board charges, and other expenses required for enrollment at almost any higher education institution. These plans are available in all 50 states. They are treated as any other parental asset under federal financial aid guidelines. This means that only 5.5 percent of the plan assets are counted toward a family's expected contribution versus 35 percent of a student-held asset, such as an education savings account or a custodial account. Now that higher education distributions from these plans are excluded from income, the distributions will not be included as student income in the financial aid formula used in determining the family's expected financial contribution to tuition and other expenses.

As good as Section 529 state tuition programs were in the past, they are now vastly better. Before 2002, earnings on prepaid amounts were tax-deferred until used to pay for the student's higher education. At that time, distributed earnings were taxable to the student-beneficiary, who was usually in a lower tax bracket than the parent or other contributor. The educational fund built up faster, owing to tax deferral, and the tax that was ultimately owed was almost always much lower than it would have been at the parent-contributor's rate.

Now, however, distributions from these state tuition programs that are used to pay qualifying higher education expenses are completely tax-free until 2010. This applies to both prepaid tuition plans and tuition savings plans. As a result, they are a *much improved* higher education savings vehicle.

Legislative Alert

The Treasury Department has proposed that the exclusion for Section 529 plan distributions used to pay higher education expenses be made permanent.

Private educational institutions now are permitted to establish prepaid tuition programs (but not tuition savings plans) that have the same tax benefits as state tuition plans.

Unlike most other tax-advantaged education savings vehicles, there are no limits to prevent high-income individuals from using 529 plans. Substantial sums can be accumulated for a beneficiary—more than $300,000 in some plans.

The private plans should be attractive to many parents and future students, especially families with a history of attendance at a particular private college. Currently, there is one organization that has created a nationwide prepaid tuition program. The Independent 529 Plan permits the purchase of prepaid tuition that can be used at more than 200 private schools.

A rollover option allows transfers between the tuition plans of different states, between a state's prepaid tuition plan and its savings plan, or between a state tuition plan and a private plan. While the federal tax law permits rollovers, plans are not required to do so. If flexibility is important, make sure that the plan permits rollovers.

What Expenses Qualify?

Tax-free qualified tuition plan benefits (both state and private) are available to fund tuition, fees, books, and supplies. Most room and board expenses for students who attend school at least half time will also qualify. To figure the amount that can be received tax-free, expenses that would otherwise qualify must be reduced by tax-free scholarship grants, veterans' benefits, tax-free employer-paid educational expenses, and amounts that qualify for higher education tax credits. Also, amounts received tax-free from a qualified tuition plan reduce the amount of education expenses that qualify for the tuition deduction discussed on page 139.

Distributions of earnings that exceed qualified expenditures are taxed to the beneficiary and are generally subject to a 10 percent excise tax. Amounts not used by the beneficiary can be rolled over to another beneficiary's account as long as the new beneficiary is a family member (including a spouse and even a first cousin), thus keeping the tax benefits working for other family members. Earnings not used for qualified higher education expenses that are returned to the contributor are taxed at the contributor's rate plus the 10 percent excise tax. Earnings that are distributed because of the beneficiary's death or disability, or because of the beneficiary's receipt of a scholarship, are not subject to a penalty. Also not subject to the 10 percent excise tax are distributions of earnings that are taxable because the taxpayer elects to take the credits or deductions described in the prior paragraph.

Observation

The Tax Code imposes a 10 percent tax penalty for taxable distributions from 529 plans that are not used for education expenses. Before 2002, these plans had to impose a penalty on refunds not used for educational expenses. Some states have not removed their plan's penalty for nonqualified use of funds. However, this should not be a factor in choosing a state-qualified tuition plan as long as the plan permits rollovers. If there are funds in the account that will not be used for education expenses, the account could be rolled over and later distributed from a plan that does not impose a penalty of its own.

Legislative Alert

The Treasury Department has recommended that Congress create legislation that would:

- Require Section 529 plans to impose penalties on distributions in excess of $50,000 that are not used for qualified education expenses.

- Require distributions by the time the beneficiary reaches age 35.

- Prevent the custodian of the account from having a beneficial interest in the account.

These rules would apply to accounts opened or contributed to after the date of enactment.

Contributions to qualified tuition plans may be made only in cash. Unlike Coverdell Education Savings Accounts, contributors and beneficiaries are not permitted to self-direct the investments in qualified tuition plans. However, most savings plans permit an initial investment selection among different investment types, and the account owner can switch investments once every 12 months and upon any change in account beneficiaries.

Many states also offer tax incentives to their residents, including state income tax deductions for some contributions to their state's qualified tuition plans. No state permits a deduction for contributions to a 529 plan sponsored by another state. Some states have changed or are considering changing the tax treatment of these programs to conform more closely to the federal tax exemption. Also, some states require a recapture of the state income tax deduction if funds are withdrawn and/or rolled over to another state's plan. The recapture is necessary to prevent the abuse of making contributions solely for the purpose of receiving state income tax deductions.

Caution

There are a number of special rules that coordinate the benefits of various tax-favored education savings vehicles. For example, if you take distributions in the same year from a Coverdell Education Savings Account and a qualified tuition program, and the cumulative distributions exceed the amount of higher education expenses that qualify for the tax breaks, the expenses must be allocated between the distributions to determine how much of each can be excluded. Also, you may claim a higher education tax credit—a HOPE or lifetime learning credit—if you otherwise qualify, and receive a tax-free distribution from a qualified tuition plan in the same year for the same student (but only to the extent that the distribution doesn't cover the same expenses for which the tax credit was claimed).

In addition to the tax advantages, Section 529 plans generally offer professional investment management. The plans of some states offer little flexibility in this regard; their investment choices are somewhat limited. In these plans, your funds usually are invested somewhat more aggressively when your child is younger and less so as the time horizon to begin paying for college nears. Other plans allow you to choose among various types of funds. However, don't expect to be able to time the market too closely. Federal tax law allows investment changes within a plan to be made no more than once a year. Since you are not limited to using your own state's plan, you can shop around and find one that gives you the kinds of investment management and choice that suits you. However, keep in mind that state tax deductions for contributions are available only to state residents who invest in their own state's Section 529 plan. To learn the details of these programs offered by the various states, log on to www.collegesavings.org/locator/index.htm or www.savingforcollege.com and click on your state.

Another thing to keep in mind is that anyone can set up a Section 529 plan. You do not have to be a parent. You can set one up naming a grandchild, nephew, or niece, or even an unrelated individual as beneficiary. If you later want to change the beneficiary without incurring income tax, you can name another family member of the original beneficiary as the new beneficiary. You will need to supply the beneficiary's social security number, but there is generally no reason that the beneficiary would have to be informed of the plan's existence. With the exception of a few prepaid tuition plans, the beneficiary has no rights of any kind regarding a Section 529 plan. Therefore, the account owner must carefully consider who will become the successor owner upon the original account owner's death. The successor owner could choose to direct the money away from the intended beneficiary.

Gift and Estate Tax Breaks, Too

Payments made into qualified tuition programs are considered completed gifts at the time payment is made into the program, even though the student-beneficiary may not receive the benefit of the gift for many years, and even though you retain control over the account. As a result, the payments are eligible for the $11,000 annual gift tax exclusion. In fact, five years' worth of annual-exclusion gifts can be made in one year to a qualified tuition plan. As a result, a married couple could give $55,000 each to the plan of the same beneficiary in a single year. However, no additional gifts from the couple could then be made to that beneficiary for the next four years without being subject to gift tax filings (see Chapter 7 for details). Furthermore, contributions and earnings in Section 529 plans generally won't be included in your taxable estate. Because of this, your education funding can do double duty as part of your estate plan.

Coverdell Education Savings Accounts

Coverdell Education Savings Accounts (formerly called Education IRAs) allow individuals to contribute up to $2,000 per year for a child to save for education. To make a full contribution, contributors cannot have AGI above $190,000 on a joint return or $95,000 if single. The contribution phases out for AGI between $190,000 and $220,000 on a joint return ($95,000 to $110,000 for singles).

Observation

The increase in the annual contribution limit makes Coverdell Education Savings Accounts much more useful. In the past, if maximum contributions of $500 were made for a child at the beginning of each year for 18 years and they earned 7.5 percent per year, the education IRA would have a balance of about $19,000 when the child was ready to start college. The increased contribution limit will increase that amount to about $77,000.

An even bigger change is that tax-free Education Savings Account distributions now can be used for kindergarten, primary-school, and secondary-school tuition and expenses as well as for higher education expenses. Qualified expenses include not only tuition and fees but also tutoring costs, room and board, uniforms, transportation, and extended-day programs. Even some computer equipment and Internet access qualifies if used by the beneficiary and the beneficiary's family during a year that the beneficiary is enrolled in school.

Any unused amounts in an Education Savings Account must be distributed before the beneficiary turns 30 or be rolled over into an Education Savings Account for another family member under age 30. Undistributed amounts are taxed to the beneficiary at that time. Eligible family members include the beneficiary's spouse, children, brothers and sisters, and nieces and nephews. If a distribution is not used for educational expenses, the beneficiary is taxed on the earnings and must pay a 10 percent penalty.

Now, the HOPE Scholarship or Lifetime Learning Credits are available in the same year in which an income exclusion is claimed for distributions from a Coverdell Education Savings Account as long as expenses for which a credit is claimed aren't the same ones for which the exclusion is claimed.

Observation

Your children and grandchildren may be able to benefit from a Coverdell Education Savings Account even if your income exceeds the AGI threshold. Anyone can establish a Coverdell Education Savings Account for your child or grandchild. Grandparents, aunts, uncles, or even siblings can make the contributions, provided their income is below the modified AGI limitation, and the IRS agrees that even a child may contribute to his or her own Coverdell Education Savings Account. Also, companies now may make contributions to Coverdell Education Savings Accounts. If a parent's income is too high to make a contribution, his or her company may make the contribution to the child's Coverdell Education Savings Account. (Such a payment would be taxable compensation to the parent, the same as if the company paid the parent who, in turn, made the contribution to the account.)

Legislative Alert

The Treasury Department has recommended that Congress eliminate the income restrictions for Coverdell Education Savings Accounts.

Observation

Parents who intend to send their children to private elementary and secondary schools may want to use Coverdell Education Savings Accounts to help pay those costs and use qualified tuition programs to build a higher education fund. Contributions to a Coverdell Education Savings Account can be made until April 15 following the end of a year to which the contribution relates.

Impact of Lower Capital Gains and Dividends Taxes

The reduced tax rate on qualified dividends and capital gains (see Chapters 1 and 2) should have little impact on the decision to participate in state sponsored college savings programs (Section 529 plans) or Coverdell Education Savings Accounts. These plans offer the potential for tax-free appreciation on stocks (dividend paying or otherwise) as long as funds are used for education.

Roth IRAs

Roth IRAs have a special distribution payout rule that makes them a good source of tax-advantaged cash for education funding. If you withdraw funds from a regular IRA to pay for college while you are under age $59^{1}/_2$, the withdrawal is mostly, if not completely, taxable. With a Roth IRA, however, you can withdraw up to the amount of your contributions tax-free for any purpose, even if you are under age $59^{1}/_2$. Earnings on the contributions are deemed withdrawn only after you have withdrawn *all* contributions. If you need to withdraw earnings on the contributions to pay for qualified education expenses, they will be included in your gross income, but will not be subject to the usual 10 percent early withdrawal penalty.

Example

John Smith contributes $3,000 a year to a Roth IRA for 10 years. At the end of that period, he can withdraw his $30,000 cumulative contribution both income tax and penalty free. Earnings on the contributions remain in the account to further compound for his retirement.

Observation

The increased IRA contribution limits that have begun to be phased in (see Chapter 3 for details) make this strategy even more useful.

Traditional IRAs

Traditional IRAs are generally not as good a source for funding education expenses as the other vehicles described in this chapter because all distributions are included in income if all contributions were deductible. (If nondeductible contributions were made, part of each distribution is taxable and part is considered to be a return of capital.) However, if an IRA withdrawal is used to pay for qualified educational expenses for you or your spouse, child, or grandchild, no 10 percent early withdrawal penalty is imposed. Qualified educational expenses include tuition, fees, books, supplies, and required equipment at a postsecondary school.

Observation

This penalty exception for higher education expenses does not apply to premature distributions from qualified retirement plans, but it does apply to simplified employee pension (SEP) plan distributions, which are treated as IRAs for this purpose.

HOPE Scholarship and Lifetime Learning Credits

Taxpayers may be eligible to claim a nonrefundable HOPE Scholarship tax credit or a Lifetime Learning tax credit against their federal income taxes for qualified tuition and related expenses.

A HOPE Scholarship tax credit provides up to $1,500 in tax credits per student, but only for each of the first two years of at least half-time college enrollment. A Lifetime Learning tax credit is also available, now providing an annual 20 percent tax credit on the first $10,000 of tuition and related expenses, for a maximum of $2,000 per year. The Lifetime Learning credit maximum applies per-household, not per-student, and can be claimed for yourself, your spouse, or your child. Note that only one of these credits can be claimed in any year for the expenses of a given student.

Students claimed as dependents may not take either credit on their own tax returns. Qualifying educational expenses that a dependent student pays are treated as paid by the person who claims the student as a dependent for purposes of calculating that person's HOPE credit. Amounts paid to educational institutions by third parties, such as grandparents, are treated as paid by the student (and, in turn, by the student's parents if they claim the student as a dependent).

If you are above the income threshold in 2004 for these credits (availability of the credits phases out between a modified AGI of $42,000 and $52,000 for singles; $85,000 and $105,000 for married couples filing jointly), there may still be some opportunities to benefit from the credits. If you forgo claiming your student-child as a dependent, and the child has sufficient taxable income to be able to use the credit, the tax value of the credit may be more than you lose by giving up the dependency exemption. There is no restriction on the type of income that may be offset by the tax credit, so a child's investment income would qualify.

Observation

The higher your income, the better this trade-off is, since your ability to claim dependency deductions on a 2002 joint return starts to phase out at $209,250 of adjusted gross income and disappears completely above $331,750. Even if you are not phased out of the dependency deduction, the 2003 Act's drop in tax rates makes tax credits relatively more valuable than they were previously. In other words, giving up the dependency deduction for a child costs you less than before, while the credit remains as valuable as ever.

U.S. Savings Bonds

You may exclude from income any interest received on redemption of U.S. savings bonds purchased after 1989 when you were 24 or older if qualifying educational expenses for the tax year exceed the aggregate proceeds received from redemption of bonds.

> ### Observation
>
> The ability to use this provision in 2004 begins to phase out for single individuals with an AGI of $59,850 and married couples with an AGI of $89,750. The phase-out range for the interest exclusion is $15,000 for singles and $30,000 for joint-return filers. Because the income level is measured in the year the bonds are redeemed (which might be years into the future), you may not be able to take advantage of the provision if income levels are too high at that time. The interest income would then be subject to tax at ordinary rates.

If you are concerned that your income may be too high in the year of redemption, it might make more sense to invest in growth stocks. This will allow you to manage the capital gains income and you could transfer the stock to your child on a "just-in-time" basis, to be sold at reduced capital gains rates (see "Income Shifting and Capital Gains," page 141).

Example

Mr. Jones redeems series EE bonds in the amount of $20,000. Mr. Jones paid $12,000 for the bonds in 1991 and would have to recognize $8,000 of interest income upon the redemption. If Mr. Jones has qualifying education expenses of at least $20,000 during the tax year in which he redeems the bonds and his income is low enough, he avoids income tax on the interest income from the bond redemption. Qualifying educational expenses include tuition and fees spent for the taxpayer, the taxpayer's spouse, and dependents of the taxpayer.

Home Equity Loans

If you need to borrow to pay college expenses, consider a home equity loan. You can claim the loan interest as an itemized deduction, up to a maximum debt amount of $100,000. However, home equity debt interest is not deductible for alternative minimum tax purposes.

Student Loans

You may deduct up to $2,500 of interest paid on qualified education loans (loans taken out and used solely to meet higher education expenses), which you are liable to repay, even if you don't itemize deductions. Interest on loans from relatives or other individuals can't be deducted.

The student loan interest deduction phases out at a modified AGI level between $50,000 and $65,000 for singles, and $105,000 and $135,000 for married joint return filers.

Observation

Due to the phase-out thresholds, many parents are shut out of this deduction because their family income is too high. If borrowing is necessary in these situations, it usually makes sense for the student, rather than the parent, to take out as much of the loan as possible to generate maximum tax benefits. The deduction is not available to a child for any year when the child is claimed as a dependent on the parents' tax return. However, the child is not likely to be a dependent when the loan is being repaid following graduation. At that time, parents can make gifts to the child to help with loan repayment.

Tuition Deduction

Through 2005 only, a limited amount of higher education expenses are deductible by itemizers and nonitemizers alike. As with most education tax breaks, those with higher incomes won't be able to claim this. A deduction of up to $4,000 is permitted in 2004 and 2005 for singles with an AGI no higher than $65,000 or married couples with income no higher than $130,000. A maximum $2,000 deduction is available for those with higher incomes of up to $80,000 for singles and $160,000 for married couples. The deduction isn't available to those who can be claimed as dependents on another person's tax return.

There are also other restrictions. The tuition deduction can't be claimed for a year if a HOPE or Lifetime Learning credit is claimed for the same student. Also, no deduction will be allowed for the part of a qualified tuition plan distribution, savings bond redemption, or Education Savings Account that represents tax-free earnings; however, the part of the distribution representing a return of capital does qualify for the deduction.

Legislative Alert

The deduction for higher education expenses and student loan interest would be replaced by a per-student, not per-household, Lifetime Learning credit with a higher income eligibility under a Treasury Department proposal.

Relatives

Relatives, especially grandparents, with taxable estates (those that exceed the $1.5 million estate allowance that applies in 2004 and 2005) may be looking for methods to reduce their estates despite additional future increases in the amounts that may escape estate tax (see Chapter 7). Payments of tuition made directly to an educational institution do not count against the gift tax annual exclusion amount. Thus, grandparents can write a tuition check directly to the school and still make an $11,000 tax-free gift to their grandchild without owing any gift tax or even reducing the amount that can be passed on free of estate tax. Even multiyear advance tuition payments may be structured to be gift tax-free.

Income Shifting and Capital Gains

As discussed in Chapter 2, the new, lower capital gains tax rates make it worthwhile to consider shifting income to your children who may pay only a 5 percent tax on capital gains.

Observation

If you expect to have capital gains from selling stock to pay for college or another major expense for a child age 14 or older, consider giving the asset to the child, who can then sell it. Assuming that the child is in a 10 percent or 15 percent tax bracket, the child will pay tax at the 5 percent capital gains rate (even if the asset is sold the next day) as long as the combined holding period exceeds 12 months. Keep in mind that both your purchase price and date of purchase will transfer to gift recipients.

Observation

Remember, the gift tax may apply to gifts over $11,000 from single individuals and $22,000 from married couples.

Observation

To fund college or other expenses for children, consider assets that are likely to provide superior capital appreciation over the minimum one-year-plus holding period. These assets can now be held in the child's name (in a Uniform Gifts to Minors Act [UGMA] or Uniform Transfers to Minors Act [UTMA] account) or in trust (as long as the trustee has the ability to distribute capital gains) or be a gift to the child on a "just-in-time" basis, since there would be a carryover purchase price and purchase date.

> **Observation**
> If qualifying for financial aid is a possibility, it may be wise to keep assets in the parents' names and transfer them to the student on a "just-in-time" basis. This is because the federal financial aid family contribution formula requires parents to contribute a smaller percentage of their assets than students must.

Employer Education Assistance

Many employers, especially larger ones, have benefit plans that provide up to $5,250 a year of education assistance to employees. This benefit is tax-free to employees if it applies to tuition and related expenses, such as fees, books, and certain associated supplies and equipment. Other related expenses, such as meals, lodging, and transportation, aren't covered by the income exclusion. The courses do not have to be job-related for the benefit to be tax-free. So, for example, a person who works as a clerk or secretary at a company could take courses toward a degree in literature, history, or economics and receive tax-free benefits. Tax-free assistance is not available, however, for courses involving sports, games, or hobbies.

An employee whose employer's plan permits can receive tax-free benefits to attend graduate school part-time while working. Tax-free benefits are not available to companies whose education assistance plan discriminates in favor of highly compensated employees and their dependents. However, union employees don't have to be covered if education assistance was the subject of good faith bargaining.

If your employer doesn't have an education assistance plan, but reimburses you for education expenses, the reimbursement is tax-free if the education is job-related, that is, if it maintains or improves a skill currently used in your trade or business, or is

Table 5.1   *Tax Breaks for Education*

Type of Arrangement	Main Features	Income Limits
Qualified tuition plans	Post-2001 (post-2003 for private plan) distributions for higher education expenses are tax-free Large gift-tax-free contributions can be made Can be transferred to other family members	None
Coverdell Education Savings Accounts	Per-child contribution limit: $2,000 Tax-free distributions for education Can be used for kindergarten through postgraduate, including school-related computer equipment purchase and room and board Broad investment choice	Contribution limit phases out between a modified AGI of $95,000–$110,000 for singles; $190,000–$220,000 for joint filers
Education savings bond exclusion	Interest is tax-free on redemption for higher-education expenses (but not room and board) Proceeds can be transferred to Coverdell ESA or qualified tuition plan Child can't own bonds	Exclusion phases out for 2004 between a modified AGI of $59,500 and $74,500 for singles, or $89,750 and $119,750 for joint filers
Student loan interest deduction	Up to $2,500 of student loan interest deductible, even by nonitemizers Can't be claimed by tax dependent	Maximum deduction phases out between a modified AGI for 2004 of $50,000–$65,000 for singles; $105,000–$135,000 for joint filers

(continued)

Table 5.1   *(Continued)*

Type of Arrangement	Main Features	Income Limits
Tuition deduction	Maximum $4,000 deduction for 2004 and 2005 only Not available if higher education tax credit is claimed for the same student	$4,000 deduction available for singles with a modified AGI of up to $65,000 ($130,000 for joint filers) $2,000 deduction available for singles with a modified AGI of $65,000–$80,000, and $130,000–$160,000 for joint filers
Higher-education tax credits	HOPE credit: up to $1,500 per student for first and second year of post-secondary education Lifetime Learning credit: per household— maximum $2,000	Phases out between a modified AGI of $42,000–$52,000 for singles; $85,000–$105,000 for joint filers
Roth IRA distributions for higher-education expenses	Tax-free after 59½ if plan established five years Distributions tax-free and penalty-free up to amount of contributions Exempt from premature distribution penalty, even if distribution is taxable	None for favorable tax treatment of distributions
Traditional IRA distributions for higher-education expenses	Taxable to same extent as other IRA distributions, but exempt from 10% premature distribution penalty	None
Education-assistance plan	Up to $5,250 of employer-provided education assistance is tax-free Does not have to be job-related education Includes graduate study	None

required to continue your employment. However, the courses can't qualify you for a new profession (such as law school courses taken by a CPA or MBA) or be needed for you to meet the minimum educational requirements for your current position.

If you pay for job-related courses on your own, without being reimbursed by your employer, you can deduct the expenses on your own tax return as miscellaneous itemized deductions. However, your expenses won't be fully deductible because you can only claim otherwise deductible miscellaneous expenses that exceed 2 percent of your adjusted gross income. If your AGI is $100,000, for example, your first $2,000 of miscellaneous expenses are nondeductible. Also, miscellaneous deductions cannot be claimed for alternative minimum tax purposes.

The tax law makes paying for college much more affordable for many (see Table 5.1 on pp. 143–144). Parents need creative ways for turning tax burdens into tuition tamers, a need that Congress has begun responding to in the ways this chapter has described.

Higher education can be a large expense for a family. But medical expenses can also be very costly. Fortunately, the tax law now provides some ways in which to pay for medical expenses in a favorable way, as you will see in Chapter 6.

Idea Checklist

☑ Fund a qualified Section 529 tuition plan, especially if your income exceeds the threshold for Education Savings Accounts.

☑ If you qualify, fund a Coverdell Education Savings Account and a qualified tuition plan if you plan to send your children to a private elementary or high school.

☑ Have lower-income family members establish Coverdell Education Savings Accounts for children and grandchildren; alternatively, have children contribute to their own Coverdell Education Savings Accounts.

☑ Shift capital gains income into a 5 percent bracket by giving stock to your children or grandchildren age 14 or older.

☑ If loans are needed to help pay for educational expenses, first consider a home equity loan.

☑ Be sure relatives know that tuition can be paid directly to an educational institution in addition to $11,000 annual exclusion gifts, and that up to five years' worth of annual exclusion gifts can be made at one time to a qualified Section 529 tuition program.

☑ Consider funding a Roth IRA so you can withdraw your contributions tax-free and penalty-free to pay for college.

☑ Be aware of the higher income thresholds for some education tax incentives to know if you qualify for any that you couldn't use in past years.

☑ Consider not claiming your child as a tax dependent if your child has enough income to benefit from a higher education tax credit.

☑ Determine whether the new lower capital gains and dividends tax rates make saving for higher education outside of special tax-qualified vehicles a viable option after taking account of financial aid implications.

Chapter 6

NEW MEDICAL COVERAGE OPTIONS

The Medicare Prescription Drug, Improvement, and Modernization Act of 2003, designed primarily to create prescription drug programs for Medicare beneficiaries, also introduced a new way for non-Medicare beneficiaries to pay for medical expenses on a tax-deductible basis. This law created Health Savings Accounts (HSAs), effective January 1, 2004.

In addition, over the past few years, the IRS has supported company plans to provide medical benefits to employees on a tax-advantaged basis by issuing a number of favorable rulings.

In the past, small businesses and self-employed individuals were permitted to set up Archer Medical Savings Accounts (MSAs). However, these accounts expired on December 31, 2003 (although anyone who had set up an MSA before expiration may continue to fund it each year or opt to roll over funds into an HSA).

What Are Health Savings Accounts?

If you receive health insurance through work or personally buy health insurance that meets the requirements of a high-deductible health plan (HDHP), you may contribute money to a savings-type account and claim a tax deduction for your contributions or you may be able to make pre-tax contributions to the HSA through your employer's cafeteria plan. If your employer maintains an HSA, contributions that your employer makes on your behalf are not taxable to you (and are not subject to Social Security and Medicare taxes). You own the account and can take it with you when you leave the company.

Funds in the account build up on a tax-deferred basis (earnings are not currently taxed). If withdrawals are taken to pay medical costs that are not covered by insurance, withdrawals are tax-free. Withdrawals for any other purpose are taxable. If you are under age 65, there is also a 10 percent penalty on nonmedical withdrawals.

Observation

Nobody monitors withdrawals from HSAs to see that they are used for medical purposes. It is your responsibility to keep receipts and other proof to show that you used withdrawals for a tax-free purpose.

Currently, more than 40 insurance companies are offering policies that meet the requirements of HDHPs and that number is expected to double before the end of 2004. HSAs are recognized in 49 states and the District of Columbia.

Eligibility

Whether you are covered by an HDHP from your employer or buy your own policy, make sure it meets the tax law requirements so you can contribute to an HSA. Premiums for an HDHP are lower than for traditional, more extensive medical insurance.

HSAs are open to anyone who, on the first day of the month, meets these requirements:

- The person is covered by a plan that meets the definition of high-deductible health plan. The person is not covered by another type of health insurance plan (other than certain specific coverages, such as workers' compensation, long-term care, disability, vision and eye care, and insurance for specific illness or disease and a few other specified exceptions).
- The person is not eligible for Medicare.

A high-deductible health plan is defined as a plan with an annual deductible of at least $1,000 for self-only coverage or $2,000 for family coverage. Furthermore, the sum of the annual deductible and other annual out-of-pocket expenses cannot be more than $5,100 for self-only coverage or $10,250 for family coverage (these dollar limits will be adjusted annually for inflation).

Contribution Limits

For 2004, contributions to an HSA are limited to $2,650 for those with self-only coverage or $5,250 for family coverage (any plan other than self-only); these limits will be adjusted annually for inflation.

For those age 55 or older by year-end, the contribution limit is increased by $500 in 2004 and increases in $100 increments up to $1,000 in 2009. Contributions are fully deductible as an adjustment to gross income. You do not have to itemize medical expenses to claim this deduction.

Like IRAs, you have until April 15, 2005, to make HSA contributions for 2004.

Health Reimbursement Accounts

Your company may credit an amount to an account set up on your behalf called a health reimbursement account (HRA). You can draw from the account to pay medical costs not covered by insurance. You are not taxed on the contributions or on the withdrawals.

Your employer may provide you with a credit or debit card to use in accessing funds in your account or require you to submit bills and receipts to obtain reimbursements. Any funds in your account that are not used by year end may be carried forward to increase your available funds in the following year.

Flexible Spending Arrangements

Your company may allow you to contribute a portion of your compensation to a medical flexible spending arrangement called an FSA. Your contributions are made on a pre-tax basis. Thus, you do not pay income tax on the salary reduction amounts you commit to the FSA.

You can access funds already contributed as well as funds you agree to contribute. For example, if you agree to a $200 monthly salary reduction amounts for 2005, you can submit reimbursement for a $2,400 expense in January 2005 (even though you may only have actually contributed $200 to your FSA).

Funds in your FSA that are not used up by the end of the year are forfeited; you cannot carry them over to the next year or take a withdrawal for any other purpose.

Legislative Alert
Congress is considering a measure to allow a limited carry forward (say $500) of unused FSA contributions to the following year.

Funds in FSAs can be used for a wide range of medical expenses, including over-the-counter nonprescription medications (e.g., antacids, allergy medications, cold remedies, pain remedies) taken to alleviate or treat a sickness or personal injury.

Observation

Withdrawals are not permitted for medications taken to maintain general good health, such as dietary supplements.

Chapter 7

ESTATE PLANNING IDEAS

The repeal of the federal death tax provides less relief from estate planning chores than most people expected. As detailed next and in Chapter 1, the federal estate tax began to phase down starting in 2002 and will be completely repealed in 2010. Amounts exempt from estate tax increase during the transition period and the maximum rate of tax on estates and gifts decreases. The gift tax phases down also but it is not repealed completely.

Offsetting those advantages somewhat in 2010, however, will be some generally unfavorable changes to the income tax rules for inherited property, especially for those people with large estates. During the phase-down period, when the exempted amount reaches $3.5 million (in 2009), complications with preexisting estate plans could arise that might cause a surviving spouse to receive no property outright. Proper planning during this period may result in large tax savings for some. Another unpleasant change is that some states may add or increase the death taxes to compensate for lost revenues resulting from the repeal of the state death tax credit. Then at the end of 2010, the repeal of the estate tax is scheduled to "sunset," returning all of the estate and gift tax rules back to where they would have been had there been no repeal.

As was previously the case, estate and gift planning strategies can still protect significant amounts of property from being subject to transfer taxes. However, there is less certainty as to what the best solutions will be. This chapter focuses on important planning ideas to consider.

How the Estate Tax and Gift Tax Work

Estate and gift taxes currently work in tandem as a unified transfer tax system with basically the same tax rates and exemption amounts applying to both taxes. What it amounts to is "pay me now or pay me later." However, as the amount exempt from estate tax increases above $1 million in the future, and the estate tax is eventually repealed, the gift tax exemption amount will be frozen at the $1 million level. In addition, the gift tax will continue, although at a reduced rate, during 2010 when the estate tax is scheduled to be repealed.

Observation

If you previously used your full gift tax exemption of $675,000, you may think that you can make an additional $325,000 of tax-free gifts (in addition to your annual exclusion gifts) now that the gift tax exemption amount is $1 million. That is not the case due to the way prior gifts are figured when calculating the gift tax owed on current gifts. People who are already in the maximum 48 percent gift tax bracket can only make $260,938 ($125,250/0.48) of additional gifts before paying gift tax.

Amounts Exempt from Tax

You may transfer $11,000 ($22,000 for most married couples) each year to an unlimited number of individuals free of gift tax. To qualify for this annual exclusion, the recipient generally must have immediate access to the gift, although some gifts in trust can qualify, as can contributions to a qualified tuition program.

Unlimited amounts can be transferred directly to an educational institution or health care provider free of gift tax to pay someone else's tuition or medical expenses.

There are even bigger breaks. You can transfer unlimited amounts to your spouse free of gift or estate tax. In addition, you are able to transfer $1 million to children and others without paying any gift tax. If you and your spouse agree to split your gifts, you can give $2 million. Annual exclusion, tuition, medical, and spousal transfers do not count against this exemption. (Special rules may apply if your spouse is not a U.S. citizen.) (See Table 7.1.)

Starting in 2004, when the estate tax exemption increases to $1.5 million, the special deduction for qualified family owned business interests, mentioned previously, will be repealed.

Table 7.1 *Estate and Gift Tax Exemption Allowances*		
Year	Estate Tax Exemption (in $ Millions)	Gift Tax Exemption (in $ Millions)
2004	1.5	1
2005	1.5	1
2006	2	1
2007	2	1
2008	2	1
2009	3.5	1
2010	N/A (tax repealed)	1
2011 and later	1	1

Gift and Estate Tax Rates

Once you have exceeded the exemption amount, the estate and gift tax rates outlined in Table 7.2 apply for 2004. Thus, the maximum estate and gift tax rate for 2004 is 48 percent. In future years, the maximum rates are as shown in Table 7.3 on page 157.

Estate tax rates may be even higher than you think because lifetime taxable gifts are added to property owned at death for purposes of computing the estate tax rate. Although, your estate will receive a credit for gift taxes paid on the lifetime taxable gifts.

Currently, the recipient of most property transferred at death receives a basis equal to the fair market value of the property as of the date of death. This means that income tax is avoided on the increase in the value of the property that occurred during the decedent's life and the recipient can sell the asset immediately and not pay any capital gains tax.

The rule is different for gifts made during life. Here, the recipient gets your basis, so if he or she sells the gift property after receipt, he or she pays capital gains tax on any appreciation that has occurred since you acquired it. On the plus side, the gift recipient gets to include your holding period in determining whether a sale by him or her qualifies for favorable long-term capital gains treatment.

Table 7.2 *Estate and Gift Tax Rates*	
For Taxable Gifts and Estates Above ($)	**Rate (%)**
1,000,000	41
1,250,000	43
1,500,000	45
2,000,000	48

Table 7.3 *Maximum Estate and Gift Tax Rates*	
Year	**Highest Estate and Gift Tax Rates (%)**
2004	48
2005	47
2006	46
2007	45
2008	45
2009	45
2010	35 (gift tax) 0 (estate tax)
2011 and later	55

With capital gains rates as low as 15 percent—and only 5 percent for children and grandchildren who are in the 10 percent or 15 percent income tax brackets—it still may be worth considering whether lifetime giving makes sense in spite of the lack of basis step-up for lifetime gifts. Be sure to consider both the income tax and the transfer tax consequences.

In 2010, when the estate tax is due to be repealed, the basis step-up (basis is increased to the property's value at the time of transfer) for assets received from a decedent will be limited. Inheritors of property from decedents dying in 2010 will receive a basis step-up that will eliminate capital gains tax on a total of no more than $1.3 million of gain that occurred during the decedent's life. Property inherited by a surviving spouse will get an additional $3 million of basis increase, allowing a total basis increase of up to $4.3 million.

Observation

The dollar limits on basis step-up will not affect smaller estates. However, it will add income tax complications to estate planning considerations for those with larger estates.

Observation

Only property transferred outright to the surviving spouse or held in a special form of trust known as a qualified terminable interest property (QTIP) trust qualifies for the additional $3 million of basis increase for property passing to surviving spouses. Many persons have estate plans in which bequests to surviving spouses are held in other forms of trusts that qualify for the marital deduction for estate tax purposes, but not for purposes of the $3 million basis increase—for example, general power of appointment trusts or estate trusts. Although these types of transfers may be adequate if death occurs before 2010, these trusts may not be sufficient if death occurs in 2010 because the opportunity to step up the basis an additional $3 million would be lost.

Observation

Historically, estate plans often provided that retirement assets or other assets that may not be stepped up be left to the surviving spouse rather than children or other heirs. Under the new law, the reverse may be desirable, since it may be necessary to use the maximum amount of step-up for post-2009 transfers to a surviving spouse. It is important to consider income tax consequences other than the step-up, such as the option to make certain IRA withdrawal elections that are available only to the surviving spouse.

An estate's executor will choose which of a decedent's assets will receive the basis increase. Donors and executors will also be required to report information about certain transfers, including basis and holding period information, to the IRS and to donees and estate beneficiaries.

Observation

If some beneficiaries receive higher basis property, other beneficiaries may be burdened with higher capital gains on the sale of the property they inherit. Planning will be needed to make the most of available basis step-up and to keep potential for family strife over this issue to a minimum.

Observation

For those interested in leaving assets to charity, retirement assets remain an excellent choice because retirement assets do not qualify for a step-up in basis either before or after the repeal of the estate tax.

Planning for Phase-Down and Repeal of the Estate Tax

What will all of these changes mean for you? They will mean more, rather than less, estate planning.

First, you will have to be sure that during the transition period from now through 2009, when exemption amounts are increasing and maximum tax rates are dropping, that your existing will and your overall estate plan still do what you intended.

Second, you will need to stay on top of future changes to the estate and gift tax rules. Most estate planning experts doubt that the new rules will be implemented as they are now written. The House of Representatives has passed bills to make the estate tax repeal permanent. Conversely, the Senate has not shown a similar inclination, at least not in the current economic environment with budget deficits projected to increase further in coming years. As for complete repeal of the estate tax—even for one year—many professionals advise not to count on it. We cannot predict how the political or economic climate will change over the next seven years—only time will tell.

Planning will be easiest for those whose estates fall below the increases in the exemption amounts through 2009, which would eliminate all estate tax liability. Many will not need more than simple wills, without even the usual credit shelter trusts, to avoid estate taxes during this time. New more complicated plans will be necessary only if these estates increase in size, if the estate tax returns to its 2001 state after 2010, or if these persons live in a state with an inheritance tax that is not tied to federal exemptions.

During the phase-out period, flexibility will be needed. Some estate planners have suggested increasing the use of disclaimers (an election to decline the receipt of inherited property) to give surviving spouses the ability to balance estate tax savings with other financial needs. Wills may benefit from contingency language that would cause alternative provisions to kick in if the expected estate tax changes, repeal, and/or reinstatement do not occur as scheduled.

There are many tax-saving ideas you can use to reduce your estate. They are particularly helpful to high-net-worth individuals. One quick way to figure out whether you need estate tax planning is to look at your net worth (what you own less what you owe) and add the face value of the life insurance you own. If the total exceeds the exemption amount, think about some or all of these planning ideas.

The sooner you act, the better because a gift made now removes future appreciation from your estate.

Example

Take the case of an individual who used his exemption to make a $600,000 gift in 1987, when that was the maximum exemption amount. He died in 2004 when the gift's value had grown to $2.5 million. Thus, he effectively removed $2.5 million from his estate by acting early. In addition, the first $900,000 of his estate is sheltered by his remaining exemption allowance ($1.5 million allowance for 2004 less $600,000 used in 1987). Had he not made the gift, his estate would have increased by $1.9 million.

Observation

Those with large estates should consider maximizing the early giving strategy using the $1 million gift tax exemption.

Draft a Will

Many people do not have a will. As a result, their state of residence generally will determine who receives their property at death and how and when the property is received. If you are married with children, in most states your surviving spouse will not receive all your assets. In addition, you will miss the opportunity to generate some significant estate tax savings for your family.

Even if your estate is less than the estate and gift tax exemption allowance, you need a will to name a guardian for your minor children.

Review How Your Property Is Owned

Unless you live in a community property state (Arizona, California, Idaho, Louisiana, Nevada, New Mexico, Texas, Washington, Wisconsin, and, under certain circumstances, Alaska), in which all property acquired during marriage is treated as half-owned by each spouse, it is important for a married couple to consider how their property is owned.

For married couples, joint ownership with right of survivorship can be the ruin of an otherwise excellent estate plan. Joint ownership with right of survivorship results in the surviving spouse automatically receiving the property at the death of the first spouse. This may be a problem if you want property to go to your children or someone else. Although no estate tax will be paid because of the unlimited spousal allowance under the existing law, there might not be enough property to fund other estate planning options, such as the credit shelter or family trust (see page 166).

An asset ownership review can also help determine whether gifts or property transfers should occur during life between spouses. This allows you to make sure that each spouse has sufficient property in his or her name alone to help fund a credit shelter or family trust.

> ### Observation
>
> This review of your assets will be more crucial than ever as exemption amounts increase over the next 5 years.

Consider State Death Taxes

The state death tax credit allowable against the federal estate tax is 25 percent for those dying in 2004. In 2005, the credit will be repealed and replaced by a deduction for any taxes actually paid to any state on a decedent's gross estate.

> ### Observation
>
> Almost all states had a state death tax equal to the amount allowed as a federal credit. This generated tax revenues for the states without actually increasing the total amount of estate tax due by decedents. The state death tax credit is an important source of revenue for many states. Some states already have increased state death taxes to make up for repeal of the credit. This issue is not yet settled but it may ultimately influence the state in which you choose to reside during your retirement.

Give Gifts

Over time, a gift-giving program can remove hundreds of thousands of dollars from your estate on a tax-free basis. You can give up to $11,000 ($22,000 if your spouse joins in the gift) to an unlimited number of people each year and you will not have to pay gift tax. These figures will be increased for future inflation. Making these *annual exclusion* gifts removes property from your estate at no gift or estate tax cost, often shifting income-earning property to family members in lower income tax brackets. Additionally, you also remove future appreciation in the value of the gift from your estate.

Furthermore, there is an unlimited exclusion for any tuition you pay directly to a school or for medical care payments you make directly to a health care provider on someone else's behalf. These tuition and medical payments are gift tax free and do not count toward the $11,000 annual gift tax exclusion. Thus, a grandparent can pay tuition directly to a school on behalf of a grandchild, pay health insurance premiums and the orthodontist for the grandchild's braces, and still give the grandchild $11,000 in the same year without using up any lifetime allowance.

It should be noted that payments by parents and grandparents to a qualified tuition program do not qualify for the unlimited tuition gift tax break. Payments by parents and grandparents to these tax-favored college savings programs do count toward the tax-free annual limit.

Observation

Tuition payments for a private elementary school, secondary school, or college all qualify for the unlimited gift tax exclusion, as long as a contribution to the school would generate a charitable contribution deduction. Room and board, books, and similar expenses *do not* qualify for the exclusion.

However, you can choose to treat a contribution for a beneficiary that is over $11,000 as made equally over five years. Thus, a $55,000 gift to a qualified tuition program for a single beneficiary in a single year can be gift tax-free. For the next four years, however, you could not give the beneficiary any additional annual exclusion gifts.

Observation

It is generally better not to wait until late in the year to make gifts. Instead, it is a good idea to get in the habit of making gifts in January of each year. In a good year, an asset that is worth $11,000 in January could be worth significantly more by the end of December. By giving early, the postgift appreciation also escapes gift tax. Even though this strategy might not have worked well during recent down years for stocks, its durability has been proven over the years. There have been vastly more up than down stock markets over the years.

Observation

The reduction to 5 percent in the tax rate on dividends and capital gains for taxpayers in the 10 percent or 15 percent tax brackets increases the benefit to a parent (who is in a high income tax bracket) of making a gift of appreciated or dividend producing property to a child over 13 years of age (who is in one of the two lowest income tax brackets). In addition to the gift and estate tax benefits associated with such a gift, the family may realize an additional benefit of reducing—from 15 percent in the parent's hands to 5 percent in the child's hands—the income tax imposed on future dividends and capital gains generated by the gifted property.

Valuation Discounts

Transfers of certain types of assets, typically a minority interest in a business enterprise, may permit the use of a valuation discount for gift and estate tax purposes (so that the value for these purposes is below market value). The value of the underlying property does not change but how the property is owned may generate discounts.

Example

The true fair market value of Asset A is $100. Asset A, for valid business reasons, is placed into a vehicle that is friendly to valuation discounts, such as a limited partnership. When all the limited partnership interests are given to children, the value reported on the gift tax return might be only $75. This represents a 25 percent discount from the underlying fair market value because of the minority interest and lack of marketability. Limited partnership and limited liability companies offer many non-tax advantages, including retention of control and some protection from creditors of the donee.

Observation

The IRS has challenged valuation discounts taken when family limited partnership interests are given away in "deathbed" transfers—those made very close to the time of an individual's death. Also, you must disclose claimed valuation discounts on your gift tax return.

If you own a majority interest in a business, you can make gifts of nonvoting shares or small amounts of voting shares that would be entitled to a minority discount that would otherwise be unavailable if passed at your death. Such gifts would not receive a basis step-up at your death but future appreciation would be out of your estate. If your lifetime gifts of voting shares brought your voting rights below 50 percent, all of your shares would be entitled to a minority discount at your death.

> **Caution**
> If you own a limited partnership, limited liability company, or nonvoting shares while still controlling the entity, you will not get a minority discount on any of the interests you own.

Consider Trusts

Credit Shelter or Family Trust

Married couples should have at least this one basic trust if their combined assets exceed the estate and gift tax exemption allowance amount of $1.5 million for 2004 and 2005. Failure to have this trust can cost your family hundreds of thousands of dollars in estate taxes that could have been avoided.

Spouses with very large estates will still need fully funded credit shelter trusts. However, the increases in estate tax exemptions will require those with relatively modest estates to reexamine the impact of credit shelter trusts. These provisions ensure that both spouses' estates get the full estate tax exemption. Their purpose is to leave trusts for children or other heirs, with the maximum that can pass to them without estate tax and to give surviving spouses only a limited interest in that portion of a decedent's estate. These provisions were designed around exemption amounts ranging from $600,000 to $1 million (to which the exempt amount previously had been scheduled to rise in 2006). As the exemption increases under the 2001 Tax Act, these arrangements will be funded with larger and larger amounts—and possibly all—of a decedent's assets, in some cases leaving nothing outright to the surviving spouse. If the surviving spouse has sufficient assets of other kinds and maximizing estate tax savings is the prime consideration this may be desirable. On the other hand, use of the credit shelter trust could cause serious financial problems for the surviving spouse.

Observation

Many wills now automatically increase the credit shelter's funding as the exemption amount rises. Avoid this by specifying in your will the maximum amount of your estate that should fund a credit shelter trust.

Life Insurance Trust

If you have a life insurance policy, consider giving the policy to a life insurance trust or having the trust purchase a new policy directly from the life insurance company. If done properly, the policy proceeds can escape estate tax.

Observation

Life insurance needs for estate liquidity may decrease as the estate tax is phased out and repealed. Nonetheless, the need will not be eliminated because of the loss of full basis step-up and the possibility of reinstatement of the estate tax in 2011. You will have to take a variety of contingencies into account in drafting and funding a life insurance trust, particularly the anticipated need by your survivors for quick access to cash.

Grantor Retained Annuity Trust

Sometimes referred to as the "have your cake and eat it, too" trust, this trust is popular because it permits you to give away future appreciation on property in the trust while retaining the property's value. You even receive an IRS-determined benchmark rate of return on the value. If the trust assets provide a rate of return over the IRS benchmark rate of return, the trust's beneficiaries will receive the excess (either in further trust or outright) at little or no gift tax cost.

Typical assets placed in this type of trust include S corporation stock, publicly traded stock, and other assets that are expected to grow quickly. The higher the rate of return, the more assets that will go to the trust's beneficiaries.

Observation

Gifts to these trusts are particularly attractive in periods of low interest rates, such as we are now experiencing, because it should be easier to exceed the IRS benchmark rate of return. This interest rate varies from month to month based on interest rates on U.S. Treasury securities.

Qualified Personal Residence Trust

You can transfer a personal residence (either a first or second home) to the beneficiaries of a qualified personal residence trust at a discount from the home's current fair market value. You can live in the home for the term of the trust and continue to take a mortgage interest deduction as well as a real estate tax deduction. When your interest in the trust ends, you can rent the home from the trust beneficiaries at fair market value rates (an excellent means of further reducing your estate).

A qualified personal residence trust is especially desirable if significant appreciation is expected in the value of the home over time. As previously mentioned, the appreciation that occurs after the trust is established can also escape estate and gift taxation.

Observation

Unlike grantor retained annuity trusts, gifts to personal residence trusts are less attractive in periods of low interest rates because the gift tax cost is higher than it would be in periods of higher interest rates.

Dynasty Trust

A dynasty trust allows you to provide for your descendants (usually your grandchildren and more remote descendants) without gift, estate, or generation-skipping transfer tax consequences to your descendants. Such trusts are typically designed to last for the longest possible period allowed by law. Typically, the trustee (the individual or entity who manages the trust assets and income) will have the discretion to pay trust income and principal to your descendants. The trusts are intended to take advantage of some part or the entire amount that you can transfer to your grandchildren or more remote descendants without incurring the generation-skipping transfer tax. This amount for 2004 through 2009 is equal to the estate tax exemption amount as shown in Table 7.1. A dynasty trust can be established during life or in a will.

Charitable Remainder Trust

If you are concerned because you have built up an asset base that is not producing sufficient cash flow for you, this trust may help. The rate of return is flexible—the cash-flow yield can be improved to 5 percent or higher on the value of your asset base. At the end of the term of the trust, the remaining trust principal will pass to charity. These trusts are tax-exempt entities. They generally do not pay income tax upon the sale of any low-basis assets used to fund the trust, as you would have to if you sold the assets yourself to reinvest the proceeds at a higher rate.

Observation

You can use some of the extra cash flow that you receive from this asset transfer and establish a life insurance trust for your family to replace the assets placed in the charitable remainder trust, which go to charity at your death. However, life insurance is not a required adjunct to a charitable remainder trust.

Observation

The income tax rate reductions and its decrease in the income tax rates imposed on dividends and capital gains diminish the benefits of charitable remainder trusts, making them relatively less attractive than they had been in the past.

Charitable Lead Trust

A charitable lead trust (CLT) provides that the charity receives the income for a period of years and the remainder goes to a family member or non-charitable beneficiary. A charitable lead trust is the opposite of a charitable remainder trust (discussed earlier). The two types of charitable lead trusts are the charitable lead annuity trust (CLAT) and the charitable lead unitrust (CLUT).

Upon creation of a charitable lead trust, the donor is entitled to an income tax charitable deduction if the charitable interest is in the form of a fixed percentage of trust assets or a guaranteed annuity *and* if the donor is taxed on the trust's annual income (i.e., a grantor trust). The tax liability can be mitigated if the trustee invests in tax-exempt securities. If the donor establishes a *nongrantor* charitable lead trust, he or she will not receive a charitable income tax deduction but also will not be taxed on the trust's income each year.

Individuals who are charitably inclined can achieve important gift tax and estate planning objectives through the use of a charitable lead trust. In return for promising to make a certain level of charitable contributions, it would be possible for an individual to transfer the property remaining in the trust at some future date, without any gift or estate tax. The CLT is particularly beneficial in the low interest rate environment that we have been experiencing in the past couple of years.

Observation

Charitable lead trusts generally benefit from income tax reductions in the same ways that would result if the grantor held the CLT assets directly. However, there are factors that now may make nongrantor CLTs less beneficial. Generally, a nongrantor CLT is entitled to an income tax deduction for the annuity amount that it pays to charity. This deduction is available only to offset CLT income. Therefore, the income tax deduction may reduce the benefit of a CLT because the value of the charitable deduction is reduced.

Intentionally Defective Trust

Transfers into this kind of trust are gifts, but the person making the gift is still liable for the tax on income earned by the trust. What is the benefit? The payment of the income tax provides an indirect advantage to the trust beneficiaries because what they receive from the trust will not be diminished by taxes owed by the trust. However, it is not considered a further gift to them. The "defective" aspect refers to the fact that the person setting up the trust is liable for income taxes. Normally, that is bad, but for high-net-worth individuals, a defective trust can save a family a significant amount of estate taxes. Further tax savings may be obtained by selling property to the trust for a promissory note. If properly structured, the growth in the trust assets that exceeds the interest rate on the note may pass to your heirs free of gift or estate taxes.

Qualified Domestic Trust

A qualified domestic trust (QDOT) is a special trust that qualifies for the estate tax marital deduction if the surviving spouse is not a U.S. citizen. Generally, the estate tax is deferred until the death of the surviving spouse, at which time an estate tax must be paid based on the value of the trust principal remaining. If distributions of trust principal are paid out to the surviving spouse before death, estate tax is also generally payable based on the value of that distribution. The QDOT principal will escape estate taxation at death if the surviving spouse dies in 2010 or thereafter. Also, any distributions of principal from a QDOT to a living spouse would remain subject to the estate tax through 2020 but would be free of estate tax in 2021. (Note: Because 2021 occurs after the December 31, 2010, sunset date, this latter provision is in effect nullified.)

Observation

It is possible to completely avoid estate tax for a QDOT established before 2010 when the surviving spouse dies in 2010 or thereafter. QDOTs, therefore, should be considered for use in the estate plan of any person married to a non-U.S. citizen.

Stock Option Trust

Consider putting your nonqualified stock options in a trust for your children. Although you must pay income tax on the value of the options when they are exercised, you may save your children a big estate and gift tax bite. Most option plans must be amended to allow this type of transfer.

Effect of Reduced Tax Rates on Dividends

The new reduced income tax rates (15 percent or 5 percent) on capital gains and dividends (see Chapters 1 and 2) also apply to trusts. The lower income tax rates on dividends are particularly beneficial for dividends that are retained by and taxed to a trust because the trust income tax brackets are extremely compressed—for 2004, trust income above $9,550 is taxed at the highest rate of 35 percent (compared with married individuals filing jointly, who do not reach the 35 percent bracket until their income exceeds $319,100).

Many trusts give the trustee the discretion to distribute income to beneficiaries (in which case the income is generally taxable to the beneficiaries) or to retain the dividends in the trust (in which case the income generally is taxable to the trust).

The relative tax brackets of the trust and the beneficiaries frequently are a factor used by a trustee in deciding whether to make distributions to the beneficiaries. Previously, retained dividends may have been taxed at the highest rate due to the compressed tax brackets for trusts. Conversely, if the trustee distributed the dividends to the beneficiaries, this income may have been taxed at a lower rate because the beneficiaries may not have been in the highest income tax bracket.

The reduction in the income tax rate on dividends for both trusts and individuals generally means that the dividends are taxed at the same rate, whether or not they are distributed from the trust. This should allow the trustee to decide whether to make distributions based on other factors, such as the needs of the beneficiaries, or the grantor's purpose in establishing the trust.

Trustee's Investment Decisions

The reduction in the income tax rate on dividends gives the trustee an additional factor to consider in making investment decisions for the trust. For example, in the past, interest and dividends generally were taxed at the same rate. Therefore, a trustee may have decided to invest the trust assets in a way that generated significant interest income. Trustees now may need to consider whether the preferential treatment of dividends warrants a change to an investment strategy designed to produce less interest income and more dividend income.

Allocation of Expenses

Generally, the trustee can choose how to allocate trust expenses among the different categories of trust income (such as interest and dividends). Since dividends and interest now will be taxed at different rates, a trustee should allocate expenses to income that is taxed at a higher rate, such as interest.

Give a Roth IRA

Fund a Roth IRA each year for family members who have earned income but who do not exceed the income limitation for Roth IRA contributions (see Chapter 3) and who do not have sufficient funds (or the inclination) to make their own contributions.

Observation

Gifts of IRA contributions are an excellent way for parents and grandparents to help their children and grandchildren accumulate significant retirement assets. The early start allows the tax-free compounding to build significant asset value.

Pay Gift Taxes Now

Under a peculiar quirk in the Tax Code, it can be less costly to pay gift taxes than to pay estate taxes after death. Individuals with large estates might consider making large gifts and paying significant gift taxes before death. You must survive at least three years after the payment of a gift tax to realize the savings. Not only will future appreciation escape estate tax, but also a lower overall transfer tax can result. With the prospect of estate tax repeal in 2010, however, the idea of paying any substantial amount of gift tax now becomes much less appealing. Very old or unhealthy taxpayers who may live more than three years after the gift are the most likely candidates for this strategy.

The bottom line is that Congress has opened a window of opportunity for taxpayers to optimize their estate and gift planning. It is important to take advantage of these opportunities as soon as possible.

Idea Checklist

☑ Review your will and estate plan to determine what adjustments are needed to benefit from changes to the estate and gift tax and to avoid potentially costly pitfalls. Especially consider whether you need to change or eliminate an existing credit shelter trust arrangement.

☑ Use asset ownership forms that maximize estate tax savings (such as limited liability companies or limited partnerships).

☑ Review the use of joint ownership.

☑ Make $11,000 gifts each year.

☑ Gift appreciated capital assets to children and grandchildren in the lower tax brackets so that they will be liable for only a 5 percent tax on their sale.

☑ Pay tuition expenses directly to an educational institution or make a payment to a health care provider. Where appropriate, consider a multi-year tuition gift.

☑ Move life insurance into a life insurance trust.

☑ Put rapidly appreciating assets into a grantor retained annuity trust or sell them to an intentionally defective trust.

☑ Reconsider the investment mix of trust assets to take advantage of lower dividends and capital gains tax rates.

☑ Set things up to take advantage of any available valuation discounts.

YEAR-END TAX
SAVING STRATEGIES

Chapter 8

QUICK PLANNING GUIDE

Before the year closes, taxpayers have an opportunity to plan some moves that can cut taxes this year. To utilize year-end strategies, a taxpayer should have a good idea of his or her tax picture for this year as well as a good estimate of what it will likely be in the coming year. Changing tax rules make year-end planning more complex. Changes for the coming year, including new rules and inflation adjustments, must be factored into any decisions.

What are the best year-end tax-saving strategies? They are those that produce the largest overall tax savings, taking 2004 and 2005 into account. There are three basic techniques:

1. Tax reduction.
2. Tax deferral.
3. Income shifting.

Tax Reduction

Tax reduction occurs when you take action that results in payment of less tax than would otherwise have been due. For example, if you switch funds from a taxable investment (like a corporate bond) to a municipal bond that earns tax-free interest or to preferred stock that

179

pays a dividend qualifying for a low tax rate, you will reduce your tax bill. Or you may want to consider contributing to a Roth IRA that can generate tax-free income instead of putting the money into a taxable investment vehicle. Another option is to shift funds from an investment, such as a money market account or CD, which produces ordinary income, to a stock fund in hopes of earning some lower taxed dividends and long-term capital gain.

Caution

When doing your tax planning, don't forget about investment fundamentals. You want to find a prudent investment balance between risk and reward, taking into account your age, your family situation, and other factors. Taxes are important, but they're far from your only consideration. Work taxes into your overall financial plan, but don't let them be the driving force behind your decision making.

Tax Deferral

Tax deferral is achieved when you earn income now and pay tax on it in the future. Your retirement plan is an example. Although your retirement investments generate income throughout the years (with some years, like a couple of the recent ones, being unfortunate exceptions), they are generally taxed only when you receive them.

Deferring the receipt of taxable income can save you money, even if it produces little or no tax savings, because you can use your money longer before paying the IRS. That means greater compounding of earnings for you. On the other hand, accelerating income, even if you think you will be in a higher tax bracket in later years, means you will pay the IRS sooner than otherwise might be required. Loss of the use of that money cuts down on the advantage you hoped to attain.

Another deferral technique is to accelerate deductions from a later year to an earlier year so that you get their benefit sooner. But don't "over accelerate" deduction items to defer taxes. Remember that to get the deduction sooner, you usually have to lay out the dollars sooner, which means you lose the use of those dollars. For example, an individual in the 35 percent tax bracket for 2004 and 2005 who accelerates a $5,000 deduction into 2004 defers $1,750 of tax. This may make economic sense if the deduction is shifted from January to December. However, it is not beneficial for long periods because the funds you have to use to generate the deduction could lose more investment income in five months than the amount you would gain from accelerating the tax deduction at 35 percent for one year. Those in the lowest two tax brackets generally should not accelerate any deductions that could be paid later than February. If you are in the highest bracket, you should not accelerate expenses that could be deferred until May. Further care should be taken because not all expenses can be accelerated without limit. Also, moving up certain deductions, such as state income taxes, could trigger the alternative minimum tax (AMT). (See Chapter 11.)

Observation

Sometimes a single move (see section on "Income Shifting" that follows) can combine tax reduction and tax deferral. By deferring income when tax rates drop from one year to the next, you will not only defer your tax liability, but you will also owe tax at a lower rate (assuming that your financial circumstances are about the same from year to year). Even without a year-to-year rate cut, you can achieve a similar result by shifting income to the later year if you expect to be in a lower tax bracket in the later year due to a change of circumstances, such as divorce or retirement.

Income Shifting

Income shifting generally involves transferring income-producing property to someone who is taxed at a lower rate. One example is giving a corporate bond to a family member who is in a lower tax bracket. For example, if you're in the 35 percent tax bracket for 2004, you will pay $350 in taxes on every $1,000 worth of taxable bond interest you receive. If you give the bond to a child or grandchild in the 10 percent or 15 percent tax bracket, tax on the interest will be cut to $100 or $150 per $1,000.

Observation

Qualifying dividends are taxed at only a 15 percent rate. If the dividend-paying stock is transferred to a child in the 10 percent or 15 percent tax bracket, the dividends will be taxed at only 5 percent.

Caution

The so-called kiddie tax (which taxes children's investment income at their parents' tax rate) keeps this family income-shifting strategy from working for children under age 14. All but a small amount of the unearned income of a child under 14 is taxed at his or her parents' marginal tax rate.

Legislative Alert

Congress is considering raising the age limit for the kiddie tax from 14 to 18. This can affect your income-shifting strategies.

Tax-saving techniques are described in Chapters 9 and 10. Before turning to these chapters, however, it is important to review how capital gains and the AMT affect your tax liability this year. For more details on accelerating deductions, see Chapter 9. For more on deferring income, see Chapter 10.

Year-End Capital Gains Checkup

2004 is a year in which many stock market investors experienced an up and down ride in the market.

Those who took profits on long-term gains will get the benefit of favorable capital gains tax rates. Investors whose gains are short term are less fortunate. Their gains are taxed at regular income tax rates. If you have current capital losses, or unused capital losses carried over from earlier years, you may be able to get some tax advantages from them. You can offset capital gains—even short term gains—and up to an additional $3,000 of other income with your losses.

For example, suppose you have a $10,000 gain on stock in a company that has done well over the year but that you think is due for a fall. If you sell different stock at a $10,000 loss you will be able to sell your gain stock and fully offset your tax liability with your loss. If you recognized a total of $13,000 of losses during the year, you could offset your $10,000 capital gain and use the extra $3,000 loss to offset $3,000 of other fully taxable ordinary income, such as interest or compensation income. If your excess losses come to more than $3,000, you have to carry them over to future years, when they can offset capital gains and up to $3,000 of ordinary income (for more details about capital gains and losses, see Chapter 2).

You have a great deal of flexibility at year-end to control the timing of investment decisions to maximize your tax savings. As year-end approaches, review your investment results. Calculate recognized gains and losses and compare them with unrealized gains or losses you currently hold. (See Chapter 2 for more information on netting capital gains and losses.)

If a taxpayer has potential capital losses exceeding capital gains realized for the year, he may want to use them to offset ordinary income to the extent of $3,000—receiving a 35 percent tax benefit—and wait to recognize additional long-term capital gains until 2005, when he will be assured of paying no more than a 15 percent rate on them.

As we said before, in making these tax decisions you must also consider your individual financial and personal situation and the economic viability of particular investments. Taxes are but one factor to consider.

Year-End Alternative Minimum Tax (AMT) Diagnosis

The AMT is a separate tax system under which certain items of income and deductions receive different—usually less favorable—tax treatment than under the regular income tax system. For example, state and local income taxes and real estate taxes are deductible under the regular tax system, but are not deductible under the AMT. The standard deduction, personal exemptions, some medical expenses, some interest on home-equity loans up to $100,000, and miscellaneous itemized deductions, which you can claim for regular tax purposes, don't reduce your AMT. Also, the bargain element on incentive stock options (ISOs) that you exercise (the difference between the exercise price and the stock's value at exercise) isn't subject to regular income tax in the year of exercise, but is subject to the AMT. You must calculate taxes under both systems and pay the higher tax bill. (For a more detailed explanation of the AMT, see Chapter 11.)

Planning for the AMT can be difficult because many factors can trigger it. If you believe that you are within range of becoming subject to the AMT, year-end strategies may help reduce your tax liability. If you are subject to the AMT, you may want to go a counterintuitive route and do the opposite of normal year-end tax planning strategies. For example, individuals subject to the AMT might benefit from accelerating ordinary income items into 2004 and deferring until 2005 deductions that are not allowed for AMT purposes, such as taxes and miscellaneous itemized deductions.

If your 2004 year includes any of the items in the following list, you may need tax planning to avoid the AMT:

- Exercise of incentive stock options (as opposed to nonqualified stock options) for which the stock is held past December 31, 2004.
- Large prior-year state or local tax balance due, paid in April 2004.
- Large fourth-quarter state or local estimated tax payment was made in January 2004 rather than in December 2003.
- Expenses that exceed 2 percent of income for investment management or tax-planning services or unreimbursed employee business expenses.
- Tax-exempt municipal bond income from private activity bonds.
- Business interests owned in S corporation or partnership form, in which these entities own significant amounts of depreciable assets.
- Large amounts of dividends or long-term capital gains.
- Interest on home-equity debt that is deductible for regular income tax purposes.
- Passive activity losses that are allowable for regular tax purposes.

Now that the three basic tax-planning strategies have been reviewed, we move on to more sophisticated techniques, starting with accelerating deductions, which is the subject of Chapter 9.

Chapter 9

ACCELERATING DEDUCTIONS

Accelerating deductions into an earlier year gives taxpayers their benefits sooner. If tax rates are higher in the earlier year, the deduction also is more valuable because it offsets income that is taxed at a higher rate. That turned out to have been the case for deductions that were accelerated from 2003 into 2002. Since those lower tax rates are scheduled (absent future tax law changes) to continue to apply in 2005, accelerating deductions at the end of 2004 usually will generate only earlier—not larger—tax savings.

Nonetheless, those who expect to be in a lower tax bracket in 2005 for other reasons may get both tax benefits from accelerating their deductions into 2004.

Your goal is to use deductions to their full potential, keeping in mind that itemized deductions provide a tax benefit only if their total is more than the standard deduction amount.

Example

The standard deduction for a married couple filing a joint return for 2004 is $9,700. If you accelerate deductions from 2005 into 2004 and it turns out that your 2004 itemized deductions total less than $9,700, your effort won't have increased the amount of deductions you can claim in 2004. In addition, you will have lost the opportunity to take that accelerated deduction in 2005 when it might reduce your taxes.

Equally important is something everyone knows but few act on— keep track of your deductions, as they occur, not six or seven months later. Nothing is more painful than trying to reconstruct credible expenses that are barely remembered. It is much easier to keep expense records current and ready for a running start on accelerating deductions.

If you determine that it pays to itemize deductions for the current year (based on the figures listed next), there are certain steps you can take to move up deductible expenses. As a general rule, you should pay deductible bills and expenses received this year, rather than waiting until next year to pay them.

If you want to move up deductions into this year, you can mail a check for a deductible item postmarked as late as December 31 and still claim it on this year's return, even though the check won't be cashed until next year. In the same way, deductible items charged on a credit card by year-end can generally be deducted on the current year's return, even if the credit card bill is not paid until the following year.

If your itemized deductions come close to the standard deduction amount each year (for 2004 the standard deduction is $9,700 for joint returns and $4,850 for singles), you can benefit by "bunching" itemized expenses in alternative years so that you can itemize every other year. Bunching strategies include planning larger charitable gifts, making January mortgage payments in December, accelerating or delaying real estate taxes and state and local income tax payments, and timing elective surgery and other medical expenses prior to year-end (though keeping in mind that cosmetic surgery is not deductible).

> **Observation**
>
> Deduction bunching works best for those who don't have recurring deductible expenses every year in excess of the standard deduction amount. For example, if you pay mortgage interest and state and local taxes each year that are more than your standard deduction amount, bunching may not help you. But if you have itemized deductions each year that are close to, but under, the standard deduction amount, bunching could work well for you. You might be able to itemize one year and claim the standard deduction the next, increasing your overall deductions and reducing your tax bills.

State and Local Taxes

State and local income taxes and real estate taxes are deductible in the year paid.

If you would benefit from accelerating deductions, consider December payments of state and local estimated taxes that are due in January. You also could move up the payment of any balance of state taxes due in April to the previous year-end, but it may be more beneficial to invest those funds for the 3½-month period, particularly if your marginal tax bracket is below 25 percent.

If you have an unusually large amount of taxable income in 2004 and will have a large balance due on your state or local return in April 2005, you should consider prepaying the amount in December 2004 so that you can "match" the state and local tax deduction with the income that generated it. This technique can help you avoid or minimize the impact of the AMT on your 2005 tax return.

> **Caution**
>
> If you are subject to the alternative minimum tax (AMT) you will lose any tax savings that result from the deduction of state and local taxes because the deduction is not permitted in calculating the AMT.

Interest

You cannot deduct all interest paid on borrowed money. There are six different kinds of interest expense for tax purposes—home mortgage (see Chapter 4), business, investment, passive activity, student loan (see Chapter 5), and personal—and the deductibility of each type is treated differently. Generally, the way borrowed funds are used determines the category of the interest expense.

Business Interest

If you "materially participate" in the operation and management of a pass-through entity (a partnership, LLC, or S corporation) or an unincorporated business, you may generally fully deduct interest on business-related borrowings.

> **Caution**
>
> For purposes of determining whether you can deduct interest, managing your investment portfolio is not considered a business. Deductibility of investment interest is more limited, as discussed next.

Also, the IRS and most courts say that interest on a sole proprietor's business-related tax deficiency is nondeductible personal interest.

Investment Interest

Interest on money that you borrow to purchase portfolio investments (such as stocks, mutual funds, bonds, and the like) that produce dividends, interest, royalties, or annuity income is deductible only to the extent that the portfolio investments produce taxable income. You may carry forward indefinitely any excess investment interest expense and deduct it against your investment income in later years. To maximize your deductible investment interest, try to match investment income with investment interest expenses. Note that such interest is not deductible to the extent that the borrowing was used to purchase or carry investments that produce tax-exempt income (i.e., municipal bonds).

You can also elect to include long-term capital gains and/or qualified dividend income as investment income against which investment interest may be deducted. If you make this election, however, these gains and dividends will be taxed at ordinary income tax rates rather than at the lower 15 percent (or 5 percent) capital gains tax rates. The effect of the election is to save tax currently on your excess investment interest expense at the capital gains tax rate. This election generally makes sense only when you expect to have excess investment interest expense for the foreseeable future.

Passive Activity Interest

Your share of interest incurred or paid on a passive activity investment is, in most cases, deductible only up to the amount of your income from all passive activities that year. A passive activity investment is generally:

- An investment in an operating business in which you do not "materially participate."
- An investment in real estate or another "tax shelter." However, renting real estate to yourself or your business won't generate passive income. In general, all limited partnership investments are considered passive activities.

You may carry forward any excess passive losses and use them to offset passive activity income in future years. Also, you can usually deduct suspended passive losses from a particular passive investment in the year you sell your interest in the particular passive investment. When there is a sale or other disposition of a passive investment in a taxable transaction, net passive losses are applied first against income or gain from other passive investments. Then any remaining passive losses from the disposed passive investment are reclassified as nonpassive and can offset non-passive income such as compensation income or portfolio income, including interest and dividends.

Example

In the year you sell your ownership interest in a real estate limited partnership, assume you have $10,000 of passive losses left after offsetting all available passive income for the year, including any gain from the sale of the real estate limited partnership. On your return for that year, you may deduct the $10,000 against your non-passive income sources.

If your adjusted gross income (AGI) is under $100,000, a special exception permits you to deduct as much as $25,000 of passive rental real estate losses resulting from interest expense and other deductions if you actively participate in the management of the rental real estate. This exception phases out as AGI increases to $150,000.

Example

You own a beach house that you rent out for the season each year. You have an agent who handles rentals, but you set the rental terms, approve tenants, make decisions involving maintenance and repairs, and hire contractors to do the work. Your personal use of the property is a very small percentage of the rental time. In this situation, you are an active participant in the rental real estate activity.

If your AGI is $100,000 or less, you may deduct up to $25,000 of losses from the rental real estate activity each year against your other nonpassive income. If your AGI is $125,000, you can deduct up to $12,500 of rental activity losses. But in any year that your AGI is $150,000 or more, you cannot deduct any of the rental real estate losses against nonpassive income.

There are even more liberal rules for investments in low-income housing and for individuals and closely held corporations that meet the definition of a "real estate professional." (See IRS Publication 527, "Residential Rental Property," for details concerning what it takes to qualify as a real estate professional.) Tougher rules apply to losses from interests in publicly traded partnerships; losses from these activities can only offset income from the activity until the interest is disposed of.

The passive activity rules are extremely complex, and if you think you may be subject to them, you should consult your tax advisor.

Student Loan Interest

There is an above-the-line deduction (these deductions are sub-tracted directly from your gross income to calculate AGI)—available even to individuals who do not itemize deductions—for interest paid on a qualified education loan. The limit is up to $2,500 for in-terest paid on qualified education loans. The maximum deduction phases out for single taxpayers with an AGI between $50,000 and $65,000, and for married taxpayers filing jointly with an AGI be-tween $105,000 and $135,000. These thresholds may be adjusted for inflation in coming years (see Chapter 5 for more details).

Observation

Many student loans have repayment terms that extend well be-yond the five-year period that had applied in the past. The re-moval of the 60-month limitation means that interest on student loans is now deductible much more widely.

> ### Example
>
> You finished college with $30,000 in student loan debt, which you have arranged to repay over 10 years. Although you were a dependent of your parents while you were a student, you will no longer be claimed on their tax return. Previously, you would have qualified for the student loan interest deduction only for the first five years of interest payments. Now, however, you may deduct up to $2,500 of interest for each of the 10 repayment years, subject to the income limits.

Qualifying loans generally include only debt incurred solely to pay the higher education expenses for yourself, your spouse, or your children or grandchildren at the time the debt was incurred. Loans from relatives do not qualify. You must be the person legally responsible to repay the loan in order to deduct the interest. You can't deduct interest that you may pay, for example, on your child's loan. Nor can you deduct interest on a revolving credit line not earmarked specifically for higher education expenses. You are also not eligible for the deduction in years when you are claimed as a dependent on someone else's tax return.

Personal Interest

Interest incurred on car loans, credit cards, or IRS adjustments or any other interest falling outside the other five categories is generally not deductible. If you can obtain a favorable interest rate, you should consider taking out a home-equity loan to pay off any of these debts. The interest on a home-equity loan of up to $100,000 can be claimed as an itemized deduction, except for the purposes of the AMT (see Chapter 4).

Medical Expenses

You can deduct unreimbursed medical expenses (including those of your spouse and dependents) to the extent that they exceed 7.5 percent of your AGI (10 percent for the AMT). Doctors' and dentists' fees, hospital bills, medical supplies, stop-smoking programs, weight-loss programs to treat obesity, and prescription drugs are deductible to the extent not covered by insurance. In addition, your payments for health insurance and certain long-term care insurance (within limits) and long-term care expenses are included as medical expenses.

If medical expenses seem likely to be close to or exceed the 7.5 percent floor this year, consider accelerating elective treatment or surgery (keeping in mind that cosmetic surgery is generally not deductible as a medical expense) and paying for it before year-end. If the floor will not be reached this year but might be reached next year, consider the opposite strategy: delaying payment of medical bills whenever possible.

Observation

Although cosmetic surgery isn't generally deductible, the costs of reconstructive surgery and of radial keratotomy to correct vision without requiring prescription lenses are allowable medical expenses.

Other opportunities if you are self-employed include the following:

- Self-employed individuals may deduct 100 percent of the annual cost of health insurance for themselves, their spouses, and their dependents.
- This deduction is not allowed for months during which you are eligible to participate in an employer-provided health insurance plan (including your spouse's plan). Note that this allowance is an "adjustment to income" rather than an itemized deduction. Therefore, it can be taken even by nonitemizers and is not reduced for itemizers at higher income levels.

- If you are self-employed you may deduct a percentage of the cost of long-term care insurance premiums, as long as you are not eligible for any employer-provided, long-term care insurance (including under your spouse's plan).

Charitable Contributions

Charitable contributions are one of the most flexible deductible expenses because you can usually control their timing and amount.

For example, you could accelerate deductible expenses by making a contribution in December rather than January. A contribution is considered made at the time of delivery (mailing a check constitutes delivery, assuming that it clears in due course). You cannot take a deduction based only on a pledge—you must actually make the contribution.

In general, you can deduct contributions to qualified charities of up to 50 percent of your AGI. These deductions are also allowed for AMT purposes. Any excess can be carried forward for five years.

Observation

Taking advantage of tax cuts may produce more disposable income that could be used to make charitable contributions. On the other hand, the rate reductions also remove some of the tax incentive for charitable giving by increasing its after-tax cost. Most charitable givers, however, have more than taxes in mind when they make their contributions.

Observation

You can establish a donor-advised philanthropic fund as a means to get a current deduction and earn a tax-free return until you wish to donate the funds to particular charities.

Donor-advised philanthropic funds can be established through community foundations as well as certain mutual fund companies and other financial and charitable organizations. The minimum contribution to establish the fund can be as low as $10,000.

Observation

Unreimbursed expenses you incur as a volunteer, including mileage driven in your car, are deductible. The mileage rate for purposes of the charitable deduction is 14 cents per mile for 2004.

Property Donations

Special rules apply to donations of property to charities. If you donate appreciated property, such as securities or land, your deduction is based on the property's current market value rather than on its original cost. Contributions of appreciated capital gains property, however, are limited to 30 percent of AGI unless a special election is made to reduce the deductible amount of the contribution.

Instead of selling property that has been held for longer than one year and has appreciated in value and then donating the proceeds, consider donating the property itself. If you sold the property and donated the proceeds, you would pay capital gains tax on any appreciation, while receiving a deduction for only the amount of cash that is left to contribute to the charity. If you donate appreciated property directly to a charity, you escape the capital gains tax and receive a deduction for the property's full fair market value.

If property that you are considering donating to charity has decreased in value, however, you should sell it and donate the proceeds. In addition to the charitable deduction, the sale will generate a capital loss that can be used to offset other capital gains and up to $3,000 of other income.

For contributions of appreciated property to a private foundation, the restriction that used to limit the charitable deduction for gifts of publicly traded stock to your tax cost basis in the stock no longer applies. A full fair market value deduction for contributions of "qualified appreciated stock" is permitted. Such stock must be a long-term capital asset traded on an established securities market. No more than 10 percent of the value of all of a company's outstanding stock may be contributed.

> ### Observation
>
> The deduction for contributions of long-term capital gains property to a private foundation is generally limited to 20 percent of AGI for any year. Any excess can be carried forward and deducted for five years, subject to the 20 percent limit.

Any charitable contribution of property other than marketable securities that is worth more than $5,000 ($10,000 for gifts of closely held stock) must be supported by a qualified appraisal completed by the extended due date of your tax return. The appraiser and a representative of the charitable organization must sign Form 8283 or the deduction will be denied. Additional requirements apply to contributions of art if a deduction of $20,000 or more is claimed.

Substantiation Requirements

The general substantiation requirements for a deductible charitable contribution are:

- **Cash contributions under $250.** A canceled check is acceptable as long as no goods or services are received in exchange.

- **Cash contributions of $250 or more.** These contributions must be acknowledged in writing by the charity. You must obtain this documentation from the charity by the date your tax return is filed or the due date of the return (including any extensions), whichever is earlier. The acknowledgment must state whether the charity provided any goods or services in return for the contribution and, if so, provide the information required for quid pro quo contributions (see the following discussion).

Observation

This rule applies only if $250 or more is given at one time. For example, if over the course of a year, you make several contributions of $200 to the same charity, the substantiation requirement does not apply.

- **Noncash contributions under $250.** The donor should retain a detailed list of the items contributed, including the estimated value of the goods.
- **Noncash contributions of $250 or more.** The donor must obtain a receipt that describes the donated property (and indicates any goods or services received in exchange). The charity is not required to place a value on the property. For noncash contributions over $500, additional information must be included with the donor's tax return.

Caution

The IRS has instructed its examiners to look closely at donations of used autos. Donate only to reputable charities and do not be overly aggressive in valuing your donated auto. Be sure to keep evidence of its condition, such as photos and maintenance records and receipts.

- **Quid pro quo contributions over $75.** A quid pro quo contribution is one that is partly a charitable contribution and partly a payment for goods or services. The charity must provide the donor with a written statement that includes a good-faith estimate of the value of the goods or services provided and must inform the donor that the contribution deduction is limited to the payment in excess of the value of the goods or services. Contributions are fully deductible if goods or services received from the charity are only of nominal value or when only an intangible religious benefit is received.

Deferred Giving

The most common form of charitable contribution is the "current gift," for which you transfer control of money or property to a charity and you keep no control over it.

In recent years, however, *deferred giving* has become increasingly popular. This involves an irrevocable transfer to a charity whose ultimate use of the property is deferred to some time in the future. For many, deferred gifts provide the best of all worlds: a current charitable deduction, a retained income stream (or a future interest in the property for your beneficiaries), a charitable contribution to a favorite organization, and a reduction in the donor's taxable estate.

If you make substantial charitable contributions each year, consider establishing a charitable lead trust or charitable remainder trust to accomplish some of these desirable results. In a charitable lead trust, you donate property to a trust that guarantees to pay the charity a fixed amount or a fixed percentage of the fair market value of the trust's assets for a certain number of years. At the end of the term, remaining trust assets revert to you or to a designated beneficiary, such as a child or grandchild.

In a charitable remainder trust, you transfer property to a trust, and the trust guarantees to pay you or a designated noncharitable beneficiary a fixed amount or a fixed percentage of the fair market value of the trust's assets for life or a term of years. At the end of the term, the remaining assets are transferred to a charity.

> ### *Observation*
> The rules for establishing these charitable-giving vehicles are complex. If you are planning to make a large gift, contact your tax advisor to discuss how they work.

> ### *Caution*
> Deductions are not allowed for transfers to charitable organizations involving the use of split-dollar life insurance arrangements if the charity pays any premium for the donor. Employers often use split-dollar life insurance arrangements to provide a substantial amount of insurance coverage for key executives or employees. Split-dollar life insurance is permanent insurance purchased under an arrangement in which the company and the individual share the cost of the policy as well as its benefits and proceeds. (See Chapter 3 for more details.)

Casualty Losses

If you have experienced a natural disaster or another sudden casualty and suffer property damage, a casualty loss deduction is available to help lessen the blow of any unreimbursed losses (casualty losses are deductible to the extent that they exceed $100 beyond insurance reimbursement). In general, the amount of the loss is the lesser of the decrease in fair market value of the property or your adjusted basis (generally, your cost less depreciation deductions) in the property. Insurance reimbursements reduce the amount of the loss. In addition, the first $100 of each loss is nondeductible. However, if several items are damaged or lost in the course of a single casualty, the $100 floor is applied only once. Finally, only total allowable casualty losses in excess of 10 percent of AGI may be deducted.

Example

Your home was severely damaged by a lightning strike, and your loss, after insurance reimbursement, is $20,000. The first $100 of the loss is not deductible. If your AGI is $70,000, $7,000 of the remaining $19,900 loss also is nondeductible. Thus, your casualty loss deduction would be $12,900 ($19,900 minus $7,000). If your loss occurs due to a presidentially declared disaster, such as an earthquake or hurricane, you can claim the loss either on your tax return for the year in which it occurred or on the prior year's return.

Observation

Claiming the loss on the earlier year's return (by filing an amended return, if necessary) may get you a refund faster, but the calculations need to be run both ways to see which choice results in the larger tax savings.

Miscellaneous Itemized Deductions

Certain miscellaneous expenses, mostly those related to employment, including job search expenses and investments (other than investment-related casualty and theft losses) are deductible only to the extent that they total more than 2 percent of your AGI. For example, if your AGI is $80,000, only miscellaneous itemized deductions totaling more than $1,600 are deductible.

Therefore, it may be desirable to "bunch" these kinds of expenses to bring the total above the 2 percent floor at least every other year.

You can generally deduct (subject to the 2 percent floor) unreimbursed payments made in a given year for:

- The cost of unreimbursed job-related education or training.
- Unreimbursed business use of automobiles.
- Subscriptions to business or professional publications (including payment for next year's subscription).
- Membership dues in business or professional associations (including the following year's dues).
- Tax preparation and planning fees.
- Investment expenses, such as investment advisory fees or a safe deposit box.

If you receive tax preparation or investment advice or certain other financial services under a fixed-fee arrangement, you may be able to take deductions this year for payments covering a period that extends into next year. If you are delaying your deductions, you will want to make these payments after the end of 2004.

Observation
Miscellaneous itemized deductions are not deductible in the AMT computation. Therefore, the AMT is a consideration when planning any acceleration of these deductions.

If you buy and sell securities, you should familiarize yourself with the definitions of *investor* and *trader*. The vast majority of individuals who buy and sell for their accounts are investors. Investors deduct their investment expenses as a miscellaneous itemized deduction, subject to the 2 percent floor and the itemized deduction phase-out at higher incomes. Traders, however, may deduct their expenses against their trading income. It is difficult to convince the IRS or the courts that you are a trader unless you do a very large volume of short-term trades.

Moving Expenses

If you relocate because of a new job or business, you may be able to deduct certain moving expenses, including the costs of transporting household goods and traveling to your new residence. For these expenses to be deductible, your new job must be at least 50 miles farther from your former residence than your old job was from your former residence.

Not deductible are premove house-hunting expenses, temporary living expenses, the cost of meals while traveling or while in temporary quarters, and the costs of selling or settling a lease on the old residence or purchasing or acquiring a lease on a new residence. Employer reimbursements of deductible moving expenses are generally excluded from the employee's gross income, and deductible expenses not reimbursed by the employer are an "above-the-line deduction" instead of an itemized deduction.

Observation

Employers often reimburse all of their employees' moving costs, including any tax liability for moving expense reimbursements, when an employee is moved for the employer's convenience. Some of these reimbursements must be reported as taxable wages.

Above-the-line deductions are subtracted directly from your gross income to calculate AGI. They may be claimed both by itemizers and by those who take the standard deduction.

Depending on your situation, the following idea checklist may provide some help in reducing your tax bill.

This chapter described many tools and techniques that can help you use deductions at the end of 2004 and future years to lower your tax bills.

Chapter 10 sets forth a tax-planning strategy called *income deferral* that can be an important part of your overall tax-planning program.

Idea Checklist

☑ If your employer offers flexible spending accounts for medical or dependent care expenses, use them. These accounts allow you to pay these types of expenses with pre-tax dollars, offering a real savings.

☑ If you have self-employment income and want to deduct contributions to a Keogh retirement plan, you must establish the plan by December 31, even though you can wait until the due date of your return (including extensions) to fund it. Alternatively, you may make deductible contributions to a simplified employee pension (SEP) plan, which can be both established and funded after December 31 (see Chapter 3).

☑ Evaluate your form of business entity. Net income from a sole proprietor business, a partnership, or an LLC may be subject to self-employment tax; however, not all income passed through from an S corporation is subject to the tax. If you work part-time for a business in addition to your full-time job, be sure you don't fall under the "hobby loss" rules; otherwise, you may not be able to take losses.

☑ Personal property taxes such as those required for automobile license plates or tags are deductible if they are ad valorem (that is, based on the value of the property).

☑ Business owners need to remember that they can deduct only compensation that is deemed reasonable for services they and their family members provide.

☑ Corporate owner-employees should consider the impact of the reduced tax rate on dividends in deciding how much to take out of the corporation as compensation and how much as dividends (see Chapter 12).

Chapter 10

DEFERRING INCOME

Deferring income from one year to the next can be a very effective tax-planning strategy, especially for those in high tax brackets, because they will save the most. For tax purposes, many two-income families qualify as high-income individuals. Almost all individuals report their income and deductions using the cash method of accounting (in which income is reported in the year it is actually or constructively received, and expenses are deducted in the year they are paid), which gives quite a bit of flexibility in using tax-deferral strategies.

The key to saving from income deferral is that income is not taxed until it is actually or constructively received. For example, if a taxpayer does work for others, he or she will not be taxed until the year in which payment is received. So, deferring billing at year-end will result in more income being received and taxed in the following year. Some examples of situations in which income deferral may be useful follow.

> ### *Observation*
> Income deferral is even more valuable when income tax rates are scheduled to drop from one year to the next. Deferring income to a lower tax year not only delays payment of tax, but lowers the overall tax bill.

Year-End Bonuses

If you expect to receive a year-end bonus or other special type of lump-sum compensation payment, you may want to receive it and pay taxes on it in 2005 rather than in 2004. Your employer can probably still deduct the bonus this year if the company is on the accrual method of accounting (which most larger companies are), as long as its obligation to pay you is established before year-end and payment occurs within 2½ months after year-end (March 15, 2005, for a calendar-year company).

> ### *Example*
> The company where you work uses the accrual accounting method, is on a calendar year, and has an incentive bonus program for which you qualify. In December 2004, the company's directors declare the bonus and set the amount of the payments, which will be paid on January 30, 2005. The result is that the company "accrues" its deduction in 2004 when it becomes liable for payment of the bonuses, but your tax liability is delayed until 2005.

> ### *Caution*
> This strategy of delaying payment of bonuses to the next year does not work for most payments to company owners. The company's deduction for payments to partners, S corporation

shareholders, owner-employees of personal-service corporations, or shareholders who own more than 50 percent of a regular corporation is deferred until the year the bonus is actually paid to the owner—so the company is unable to accrue its deduction for the year in which the bonus was declared if it is not paid until the following year.

Deferred Compensation

You may want to consider an agreement with your employer so that part of your earnings for this year are paid to you in the future, perhaps over several years. This will delay your tax obligation. If you can wait until you are retired to receive the deferred compensation, you may be in a lower tax bracket, further reducing your tax bill on that income. In this type of arrangement, interest is often added by the company to compensate you for the delay in receiving the money.

The postponed compensation will not be taxed to you or be deductible by your employer until you actually receive it. But Social Security tax and Medicare tax are generally due when the income is earned. If you are already over the FICA wage base for the year ($87,900 for 2004), you won't owe any additional Social Security tax, but you and your employer will each owe the 1.45 percent Medicare tax on the deferred amount. No additional Social Security or Medicare tax will be owed in the future when you receive the deferred compensation.

Caution

Today's low tax rates on compensation, dividends, and capital gains might cause executives to think twice before deferring salary or bonuses into nonqualified deferred compensation

(continued)

Continued

plans. Payments from a deferred compensation plan are treated as fully taxed ordinary income, and rates may be higher at the time the payments are received. Thus, executives who elect to defer compensation forgo the opportunity to receive capital gains and dividends on investments they might have made with post-tax dollars outside of the plan.

Caution

Executives also may question the premise that nonqualified deferred compensation provides an opportunity to shift income to retirement years, when they likely will be subject to a lower marginal tax rate. With marginal income tax rates relatively low from a historic perspective, executives also may question whether rates are likely to increase in the future, potentially subjecting their deferred compensation to higher tax rates at the time of distribution.

Unlike a qualified retirement plan, which generally must cover a broad range of employees, this nonqualified type of deferred compensation arrangement can usually be made for an individual employee. If you are interested in a deferred compensation plan, you should discuss it with your employer without delay because such a plan can only cover income you earn in the future, not that which you have already earned.

Caution

When you defer compensation, you are treated as a general creditor of your employer. If your employer goes into bankruptcy, you could lose your deferred compensation.

Stock Options or Stock Appreciation Rights

If you have nonqualified stock options or stock appreciation rights, in most cases, you will have taxable compensation income when you exercise them. Delay exercising them until next year if postponing income would be to your advantage.

Caution

By waiting to exercise their options, employees forgo the opportunity for capital gains on the underlying shares (any increase in the value of stock related to a nonqualified option will be taxed as ordinary income) and the right to receive dividends, both of which receive preferential tax treatment. However, they also receive the leverage effect of being able to participate in the appreciation in the underlying stock without committing capital. Therefore, despite the potential for lower tax rate dividends and capital gains, an analysis of exercise timing generally reveals that employees continue to be better off postponing exercise until later years. This may change, however, depending on assumptions regarding future income tax rates and the price behavior of the underlying stock.

If you have incentive stock options (ISOs), exercising them does not result in compensation income if the ISO stock is held for required periods (at least two years after option grant and one year after exercise). If you meet these requirements, you won't owe any tax until you sell the option stock, and then your gain will be taxed at favorable capital gains rates. However, the spread between the option price and the fair market value at the time you exercise the option is added to your income for AMT purposes. (See Chapter 2 for a discussion of ISOs.)

Caution

If you are a "corporate insider" as defined under Securities and Exchange Commission rules, you should contact your financial and/or legal advisor because you are subject to special limitations on the sale of your option stock. (See Chapter 2 for more details on stock options.)

Treasury Bills and Bank Certificates

If you invest in short-term securities, you can shift interest income into the next year by buying Treasury bills or certain bank certificates with a term of one year or less that will mature next year. If you buy a bank certificate, you must specify that interest be credited only at maturity.

Dividends

If you have a voice in the management of a company in which you own stock, you may want to take steps to see that dividends are paid in January of 2005 rather than in late 2004. This will shift your tax liability on the dividends to 2005, since you won't receive the dividend income until the later year. This assumes that the preferential tax rate on qualifying dividends will not be legislatively repealed in 2005.

Installment Sales

You generally owe tax on profits from the sale of property in the year in which you receive the sale proceeds. To defer income from a sale of property, consider an installment sale, in which part or all of the proceeds are payable in the following year or later. In that case, tax will be owed as you receive the payments. Part of each payment you receive will be a tax-free return of your cost or basis, part will be interest taxed at regular income tax rates, and part will be capital gain. Make sure that future payments are secured and that interest is paid on any unpaid balance.

> ### Caution
>
> If the property being sold has been depreciated, usually some of the gain will be taxed, or recaptured, at regular income tax rates. This recapture gain is subject to tax in the year of sale, even if you elect installment reporting. That is true even if you don't receive any payment in the sale year. So, be sure to get enough up-front cash at least to cover your tax liability on recapture income.

You need not decide to report 2004 deferred payment sales on the installment method until you file your 2004 tax return (in 2005). This gives you more time to decide whether to be taxed on profits in 2004 or in 2005 and later years. If you choose not to report on the installment method, you must elect out of it. If you do elect out, you could be liable for tax on income that you will not receive until later years.

> ### Caution
>
> Special rules limit the use of the installment method. For example, inventory items and publicly traded stock do not qualify for installment-sale reporting. Also, installment notes in excess of $5 million may be subject to an interest charge by the IRS.

U.S. Savings Bonds

Many people are aware that the interest earned on series EE U.S. savings bonds is tax-deferred for up to 30 years. However, many

people are not familiar with the newer *series I U.S. savings bonds.*
Series I bonds provide the same tax-deferral opportunities as series
EE bonds. The major difference between these two bonds is the way
the interest is calculated. Series I bonds pay an interest rate that is
indexed for inflation.

Observation

The series I bonds are one of a very limited number of investments whose return is guaranteed to keep pace with inflation.
Both EE and I bonds can be bought at your bank in various de-
nominations. Purchases of these bonds are limited to $30,000
per person per year.

Annuities

You can defer current investment income you now earn, such as
stock dividends, bond interest, and interest on savings and money
market accounts, by transferring the funds into deferred annuities,
which shelter current earnings from tax. You won't owe tax on a deferred annuity until payouts begin. However, to get this benefit, you
generally have to tie up your funds until you are at least 59½. Similar
to IRAs, deferred annuities will incur a penalty tax on premature
withdrawals, subject to certain exceptions.

Caution

Since earnings from deferred annuities are subject to ordinary
income tax when received, they don't benefit from reduced
rates on dividend and capital gain income. There has always
been a school of thought that only long-term periods of
deferral would justify the use of deferred annuities (since
they can convert lower tax-rate income into higher tax-rate
income). The reduced tax rate on dividends and long-term

capital gains makes variable annuities invested in equities even less attractive.

For portfolios that produce significant short-term capital gains or ordinary income, however, annuities may remain attractive, especially for those far from payout status. And younger taxpayers should continue to consider these investments, since long periods of tax deferral may overcome the other disadvantages.

Individual Retirement Accounts

If you earn compensation or self-employment income, you can establish a Roth IRA or a regular IRA, assuming you meet income requirements. (See Chapter 3 for more information about IRAs.) Although your income level may disqualify you from getting the maximum benefits from these savings vehicles, you may still find some limited advantages. For example, even though you may not be able to deduct contributions to a regular IRA or qualify for the potential tax exemption of a Roth IRA, you may make nondeductible contributions to a traditional IRA no matter how high your income is and benefit from tax-deferred earnings until you withdraw your money, usually at retirement.

Caution

Like deferred annuities discussed above, the earnings from nondeductible traditional IRA contributions are subject to ordinary income tax when received, and therefore, don't benefit from reduced rates on dividend and capital gain income. However, if the scheduled "sunset" of the lower dividends and capital gains rates occurs in 2009, and these rates are not made permanent, taxpayers who passed on nondeductible IRAs for several years will not be able to make up those contributions.

401(k) Plans

401(k) plans are qualified retirement plans established by an employer under which employees can defer up to $13,000 of their compensation income in 2004 or $14,000 in 2005 (these limits are higher for those age 50 or older). As with an IRA, the earnings are not taxed until they are withdrawn. Contributions to these plans are made on a pre-tax basis, meaning that you aren't currently hit with income tax on the amount you contribute. That makes it easier for you to put more money into your account. (Social Security taxes, however, are owed on amounts you elect to defer to your 401(k) account.) Also, many employers match a portion of employee deferrals. Many 401(k) plans allow you to borrow from your accounts before retirement if the loan is repaid on a regular schedule. (See Chapter 3 for further discussion of 401(k) plans.)

Shifting Income to Family Members

Shifting income to children or other family members in lower tax brackets is an excellent long-term planning strategy for high-income individuals. As a general rule, family income shifting should be done early in the year to get the most tax savings. It is never too early to begin planning for 2005 and later years.

Children age 14 or older are taxed at single individual tax rates (10 percent on the first $7,150 of taxable income and 15 percent on higher amounts up to $29,050 in 2004). You can also shift capital gains income from your 15 percent capital gains tax rate into a child's lower 5 percent rate (see Chapter 2).

The issue of who actually controls the funds—you or your child or grandchild—can determine the success of strategies that seek to use a child's lower tax rate. If you keep too much control over the transferred asset, the IRS may say you really haven't transferred it for tax purposes and will tax you on its income or sale.

The easiest way to effectively shift income is to use a custodial account, either a Uniform Gifts to Minors Act (UGMA) or a Uniform Transfers to Minors Act (UTMA) account. Keep in mind that state laws typically give the child access to UGMA/UTMA funds at age 18 or 21.

Observation

A few states, such as Alaska, California, and Nevada, allow these accounts to continue to age 25 under certain circumstances, as opposed to the cut-offs at 18 or 21 in most other states.

If you want to limit your child's access to the transferred assets beyond what an UGMA/UTMA account permits, consider a trust. But be wary of trust tax brackets. For 2004, the 15 percent bracket stops at $1,950 of taxable income, and the top bracket starts at $9,550. Also, trusts don't qualify for the 10 percent tax rate that applies for individuals. However, the new lower 15 percent tax rate on dividends and long-term capital gains, which applies to trusts as well as individuals, could mitigate most of the negative impact of these compressed tax brackets.

If you are planning to shift income to children under age 14, keep in mind that a kiddie tax is imposed on their unearned income (such as interest, dividends, and capital gains) over $1,600 in 2004. This income is taxable to the child at the highest tax rate of his or her parents. However, there are techniques that you can use to shift income to your children and avoid the kiddie tax.

You are permitted to shift enough assets to a child under the age of 14 to produce up to $1,600 of total 2004 unearned income (see Chapter 13 for the 2005 amount). The first $800 of that unearned income will be offset by the child's standard deduction, and the next $800 is taxed at the child's 10 percent rate.

Example

A six-year-old child has $1,950 of interest income in 2004 and no earned income. His or her 2004 standard deduction of $800 is allocated against his or her unearned income, and the remaining net unearned income is $1,150. The first $800 of the remaining $1,150 is taxed at the child's tax rate. The remaining $350 is taxed at the parents' top tax rate.

Unearned income	$1,950
Less: Child's standard deduction	−800
Remaining unearned income	1,150
Less: Amount taxed at child's rate	−800
Remaining taxed at parents' top tax rate	$ 350

Observation

A transfer of assets that produces $1,600 of income to a child under the age of 14 can save a family in the 35 percent tax bracket $480. When interest rates and investment rates of return are low, transfers of substantial assets can be made without going over the $1,600 unearned income limit. Note that asset transfers should be coordinated with the gift tax rules. (See Chapter 7 for a discussion of this strategy.)

Another technique is to transfer assets that generate little or no current taxable income. For example, consider giving a child under the age of 14:

• Growth stocks or growth-stock mutual fund shares.

• U.S. series EE and series I savings bonds (the interest on which may be tax deferred).

• Tax deferral products, such as annuities and variable life insurance contracts.

• Closely held stock of a C corporation.

These assets can be converted into investments that produce currently taxable income after the child is age 14 because income and any capital gains recognized on the conversion will be taxable at the child's tax rate. The tax rate is usually 15 percent for ordinary income and only 13 percent on the first $7,150 of taxable income in 2004 (see Chapter 13 for 2005 amount) and 5 percent (zero percent in 2008) for qualifying dividends and long-term capital gains.

Caution

Savings bonds held in your name may qualify for tax-free treatment when used to pay for your child's college education. If you transfer these bonds to your children, this exclusion will be lost. Because of income limitations on this tax-free treatment of savings bonds, however, it is not available to high-income or many middle-income individuals. Even if loss of the education tax break isn't a factor for you, it is still a good idea to purchase new savings bonds for children rather than transferring your own bonds to them. That's because you would be taxed on the bond's accrued interest as of the transfer date. Unless the bonds are very new and the accrued interest amount is small, it is better to start with new bonds in the child's name.

Chapter 11 discusses a topic that has affected many more taxpayers than in prior years: alternative minimum tax. Even if you have not already been required to pay alternative minimum tax, there is an increasing likelihood that you will be paying alternative minimum tax in the future.

Chapter 11

ALTERNATIVE MINIMUM TAX (AMT)

The alternative minimum tax (AMT) is a parallel tax system to the regular income tax system, but generates an alternative tax liability by: applying different rules for determining alternative taxable income; basically incorporating a flat tax rate; and limiting or eliminating the benefit of certain tax deductions and credits. As a result, the regular income tax rate reductions enacted in recent years are not fully realized by taxpayers who find themselves subject to AMT.

To avoid becoming an AMT target, a taxpayer must first recognize that AMT planning is a complicated task that requires exceptional foresight. AMT planning might result in a suggestion that you accelerate your income and defer your deductions, which is in direct contradiction to familiar income tax planning practices.

An inadequate understanding of tax rules and their potential impact on your wealth goals and strategies could jeopardize your assets and long-term plans. Therefore, it is very important to explore and plan for the AMT by running your numbers under both the regular tax and AMT system for the current year and for several years into the future. Focusing on the proper management of your overall tax liability for more than simply the next year is essential.

In some instances, an AMT planning strategy may cause an increase in regular tax. Accordingly, a key factor to consider in AMT planning is the breakeven point where an individual's regular tax and AMT are approximately equal.

With diligent and thorough planning efforts, the effects of AMT can be lessened.

Understanding the AMT

As previously mentioned, the AMT is a separate, but parallel tax system to the regular income tax system. It has its own set of rates and its own rules for deductions, which are usually less generous than the regular rules. Both systems require a calculation of annual taxes, and the taxpayer must pay the tax under whichever system produces the higher amount. The AMT system includes, in general, a broader base of income due in large part to a smaller range of allowable deductions. The favorable tax treatment available under the regular tax system is curtailed for the AMT by a system of adjustments and preferences. So, if you typically claim deductions, or have tax preference items or other adjustments, you may crunch the numbers under both regular tax and AMT and find that you are required to pay tax under the AMT system. Tax preference items or adjustments include, but are not limited to: state and local income taxes, real estate tax taxes, miscellaneous itemized deductions such as investment expenses and tax preparation fees, certain tax exempt interest income, some depreciation expenses, the difference between AMT and regular tax gain on the sale of property, and nontaxable income on the exercise of incentive stock options.

Planning for AMT can be difficult because many factors can trigger it. If you believe that you are within the range of AMT, it may make sense to consider formulating year-end tax planning strategies geared toward reducing AMT rather than the regular tax. Again, the factors contributing to both regular tax and AMT must be considered.

AMT was first instituted in 1969 and was designed to ensure that high-income taxpayers, who had historically benefited from various tax preference items under the regular tax system, pay at least a minimum amount of tax each year. As mentioned, the AMT system acts on the premise that the taxpayer should pay the higher of the regular or minimum tax.

According to the National Taxpayer Advocate's Annual Report to Congress, the AMT "will absent a change of law, affect more than 30 million taxpayers by 2010." So, why are there exponential projected increases in AMT? The regular tax system—including the personal exemptions, standard deduction, and tax rate brackets—is adjusted to account for inflation. The AMT rates and threshold exemptions have not been indexed for inflation since the Tax Reform Act of 1986. The AMT exemption amount has been increased slightly, but not enough to allow taxpayers subject to AMT to benefit fully from the reductions in regular income tax rates. As the space between the two tax systems has compressed, it has become correspondingly easier to become a target of AMT.

The net effect is that, over time, more and more taxpayers will have an AMT liability that exceeds their regular tax liability as a result of the absence of inflation indexing. The reality for many taxpayers is that the AMT is unavoidable, and therefore the key to planning for AMT is to run the numbers carefully and plan for the long term.

AMT Computation

Under the AMT system, a taxpayer must determine the alternative minimum taxable income (AMTI—which is the equivalent of the adjusted gross income under the regular tax system) using the separate AMT rules, and then apply the AMT rates to the AMTI to determine his or her tentative minimum tax. Generally, if the taxpayer's tentative minimum tax exceeds the taxpayer's regular tax, the excess of the tentative minimum tax over the regular tax becomes the taxpayer's AMT.

Observation

The basic formula for calculating AMT is as follows:

- Start with regular taxable income;
- Plus any personal exemption amount claimed;
- Plus any disallowed itemized deductions, including medical and dental (7.5 percent deduction less 10 percent deduction); state and local taxes; certain home equity interest; the bargain element on incentive stock options (ISOs) that you exercise; and miscellaneous itemized deductions;
- Subtract itemized deductions that cannot be claimed on Schedule A because of certain limits for high-income individuals (i.e., the phase-out amount);
- Subtract refunds for state and local taxes;
- Adjust taxable income for specific tax preference and other adjustment items to arrive at AMTI;
- Subtract the AMT exemption amount (i.e., $40,250 for single or head of household, $58,000 for married filing jointly or qualified widower, $29,000 for married filing separate);
- Multiply the AMTI by the AMT rate (i.e., 26 percent up to $175,000 and 28 percent thereafter);
- Subtract AMT credits; and
- Compare with regular tax and pay AMT to the extent it exceeds regular tax.

This formula should only be used to estimate the amount of your AMT liability. In order to determine your actual liability, you must calculate the liability using a series of IRS forms.

The More the Not-So-Merrier

Taxpayers who are more susceptible to the AMT include those with significant long-term capital gains and dividend income that are subject to preferential low-income tax rates, and/or have tax preference or other adjustment items. AMT taxpayers can be retirees, taxpayers with high state tax deductions (such as New York, California, and DC), corporate executives with a large amount of ISOs being exercised, and business owners with large depreciation deductions or net operating losses, among others. By reducing the regular tax rates, the 2003 Tax Act increased the likelihood that more and more taxpayers will be subject to the AMT.

While the AMT exemption is not adjusted for inflation, the 2003 Tax Act increased the AMT exemption amount as discussed above. In addition, when taxable income reaches a certain level, the benefit of this exemption must be reduced or phased-out, creating greater likelihood that the AMT will apply to a lot of surprised and unhappy taxpayers.

The 2003 Tax Act did not alter the income levels at which the AMT exemption begins to phase-out. For married individuals filing jointly or surviving spouses, the phase-out begins at AMTI of $150,000 and ends at $382,000. For singles or head of households, the phase-out range is $112,500 to $273,500. For married filing separately, the phase-out range is $75,000 to $191,000.

The phase-out of the AMT exemption amount results in $1.25 of additional AMTI for every dollar earned in the phase-out range. In the phase-out range, the marginal AMT rate on ordinary income could be 35 percent, which may be higher than the regular tax rate. Additionally, the marginal AMT rate on capital gains in the phase-out range could be 22 percent, rather than 15 percent. This means that, in some cases, AMT planning requires just the opposite action than generally suggested. That is, in this phase-out range, effective AMT planning may suggest the deferral of income and acceleration of deductions.

Observation

Top-Ten Items That May Cause AMT

An increasing number of individuals are becoming subject to the AMT. As previously mentioned, reasons for the expected swell in the number of AMT taxpayers include the lack of inflation adjustments to rate brackets and exemption amounts and the disallowance of deductions for state and local taxes. If your calendar year includes any of the items in the following list, you may need tax planning to avoid the AMT:

1. Incentive Stock Options (ISOs), triggering an AMT preference.

2. A transaction that creates significant long-term capital gain income taxed at preferential rates, relative to ordinary income.

3. Investments generating significant qualified dividend income taxed at preferential rates, relative to ordinary income.

4. Location, location, location . . . paying tax to states with high income or property taxes, such as New York, California, and DC.

5. A significant net operating loss from a flow-through entity.

6. Expenses that exceed 2 percent of income for investment management or tax-planning services or unreimbursed employee business expenses.

7. Tax-exempt municipal bond income from private activity bonds.

8. Owners of businesses operating as S corporations or partnerships that flow through tax attributes to the owner, including AMT adjustments from the business (e.g., depreciation).

9. Passive activity losses that are allowable for regular tax purposes.

10. Interest on home-equity debt that is deductible for regular income tax purposes.

An Unpleasant Surprise for Many

Although the AMT is primarily intended to ensure that wealthy taxpayers pay at least some income tax, it applies to all taxpayers. Year-end may bring an unpleasant surprise to many unsuspecting individuals. As mentioned before, the reduction in marginal rates and the lack of inflation adjustments to AMT rates has dramatically increased the number of individuals subject to the AMT. As a result, the time to start planning is now.

If you believe you will be subject to AMT this year, you may want to go a counterintuitive approach and do the opposite of the normal year-end planning strategy. For example, AMT planning frequently focuses on shifting more income to the tax year in which AMT applies and deferring deductions to the next year. This accelerated income is taxed at the 26 percent or 28 percent AMT rate (rather than the higher regular income rates that may apply in a year in which no AMT is anticipated). Deferring deductions until the next year may result in a 35 percent tax benefit (compared to no tax benefit at all in the current year to the extent AMT applies). However, both of these strategies presume that the AMT will not apply in the succeeding year, which may not be the case. As illustrated below, entirely different tax planning strategies may need to be considered if the AMT is expected to apply in successive years.

In deciding on the right strategy for you, it is essential to compute both your regular tax and AMT liabilities. These calculations serve as the basis to manage income and deductions (to the extent one is able) in order to lessen the AMT bite in a given year.

Because of the vast projected increases in AMT taxpayers for 2004, it is crucial to start income tax planning as soon as possible. Since many AMT tax planning strategies are based on the careful timing of income and deductions, it is important that your plan include multiple year calculations to disclose the full impact of the reversal of timing differences (i.e., accelerating income or deferring deductions).

Perform a year-end diagnosis to see if you may fall prey to the AMT, and if you believe you may be affected, you should discuss your AMT situation with a professional tax advisor.

AMT Planning Strategies

If you believe you are a target for AMT, what can you do? The following are two lists of the common individual tax planning items to consider, preferably under the guidance of a professional tax advisor, depending on whether you anticipate being subject to AMT in just the 2004 tax year or whether you expect to be subject to AMT in 2004 and beyond.

Observation

Taxpayer in AMT in 2004 Only

- Postpone the payment of deductions that yield no tax benefit when a taxpayer is subject to AMT.
- Possibly postpone the payment of deductions that yield some tax benefit when a taxpayer is subject to AMT.
- Consider strategies to accelerate ordinary and short-term capital gain property income in 2004.
- Reevaluate the after-tax returns from investments.
- Take prepayments of salary and bonus.
- Consider whether any exercised incentive stock options should be disqualified before year-end to minimize AMT liability if the stock has dropped in value.
- Dispose of investments in private activity bonds.
- Consider intra-family transactions.

Taxpayer in AMT in 2004 and Beyond

- Recognize capital losses if capital gains are causing a phase-out of AMT exemption.

- Pay off home equity loans where the borrowed funds were not used to improve the residence.
- Dispose of investments in private activity bonds.
- Consider making shifts in the investment asset allocation.
- Consider IRA and/or pension distributions.
- Consider intra-family transactions.

You may also want to take into account the impact of available annual tax elections that may affect the timing of income or deductions. Additional tax planning strategies would apply to taxpayers who fall under the regular tax for 2004, but expect to be in AMT in future years.

The above-mentioned suggested planning items notwithstanding, it is anticipated that AMT will remain a problematic area for family business owners and corporate executives, as well as many other higher income taxpayers. The inadvertent impact of AMT on the larger taxpayer population has yet to be fully appreciated and addressed by Congress. Is an AMT solution forthcoming?

Legislative Alert

There have been many proposals put forth in the past several years to reform the AMT system; however, it appears unlikely that any substantive changes will be made in the near future. Congress approved a one-year extension of the increase in exemption amounts for the AMT.

One barrier to successfully addressing the AMT problem is its technical complexity. AMT is difficult to comprehend and may arise due to numerous variables. Politicians are likely to be hesitant to confront the AMT issue because they lack the certainty of a directly correlated political outcome. The application of AMT to tens of millions of unsuspecting individual taxpayers in the next five years should have some political impact. These taxpayers—many of whom may not consider themselves high-income earners—are likely to exert political pressure on their elected representatives. Another barrier is that the cost of changing the AMT would be enormous and could increase the federal deficit.

Chapter 12 goes beyond the personal strategies discussed in the previous chapters and provides many additional considerations that can generate tax savings for business owners and their companies.

Chapter 12

YEAR-END PLANNING FOR BUSINESS OWNERS

Year-end planning for business owners incorporates all of the personal strategies previously discussed, but doesn't end there. There are many additional considerations that can generate tax savings for business owners and for their companies.

Business tax savings of sole proprietorships put more money directly in the hands of the business owner. When the business is operated as a pass-through entity—an S corporation, partnership, LLC, or LLP—year-end business tax planning must be done at both the entity and the individual levels to enhance potential benefits. That is because these entities don't generally pay income taxes on their earnings. Rather, income, deductions, and credits are passed through to their owners and reported on the owners' returns. Individual owners of these types of entities, therefore, need to consider the individual year-end tax planning already outlined in previous chapters and also consider planning designed to benefit the owners' individual tax position and yet complement the company's business goals. It is not an easy task, but it is potentially quite rewarding: For each $1,000 of income that a pass-through business defers or each $1,000 of accelerated deductions, the owner in the top federal income tax bracket will save $350 of current federal income tax. One hundred thousand dollars of combined company year-end income/deduction shifting reduces current income tax by $35,000 ($1 million reduces it by $350,000). There are potential payroll tax and state and local income tax savings as well. Furthermore, there may be more opportunities for income deferral or deduction acceleration at the business level than at the individual level.

The individual income tax situations of owners of businesses that are operated as C corporations are not as directly affected by the company's year-end tax strategies as are owners of pass-through businesses. But in those cases, money saved by the C corporation's successful tax planning result in more capital available for the everyday use of the business, for expansion or for dividend payments. The 2003 reductions in the long-term capital gain and dividend tax rates, however, make it imperative for C corporation owners to reevaluate whether to operate as S corporations. In many cases, the current tax regime will make it more attractive to elect to be an S corporation by practically eliminating the prior C corporation federal tax rate advantage on ordinary income. In addition, S corporations provide a substantial tax rate advantage for both long-term capital gains and dividends since they can pass through capital gains and dividends to shareholders undiminished by entity-level taxation. The factors to be considered in making this decision are spelled out later.

This chapter lays out the details on these and other year-end planning opportunities for business owners, including those for retirement plans, bonuses, and deferred compensation. It also shows how the personal holding company tax has been made much less onerous and suggests that tax planning should extend well beyond year-end to the ultimate disposition or continuation of the business.

Business owners should consult with their tax advisors and consider whether the following planning opportunities would be beneficial for themselves and their companies.

Year-End Edge for New Depreciation and Expensing Allowances

Traditionally, one of the most important year-end decisions is related to investing in capital expenditures. In 2004, there is an extra tax incentive to put business property in service—an immediate deduction equal to 50 percent of its cost. The new deduction was enacted as part of the 2003 Tax Act, which increased the existing 30 percent extra first-year depreciation allowance that was introduced by the Job Creation and Worker Assistance Act of 2002. It is meant to provide an incentive for businesses to start spending to help stimulate the economy. Regular depreciation deductions on business property placed in service in the last quarter of the year are reduced drastically if more than 40 percent of nonrealty business assets are placed in service in that quarter. However, the "bonus" or "special" depreciation allowance is available no matter how much property is placed in service near year-end.

Under the general depreciation rules for income tax purposes, business property other than real estate generally is treated as having been placed in service at the middle of the year, regardless of the actual date it was purchased and placed in service.

That's known as the *half-year convention.* For five-year business property, it results in a 20-percent first-year depreciation allowance. If too large a portion of nonrealty business assets is placed in service in the fourth quarter, however, each asset is treated as having been placed in service in the middle of the quarter in which it was placed in service. This is called the *mid-quarter convention.* For five-year property, it could result in a depreciation deduction of only 5 percent. But, as mentioned earlier, the special 50-percent depreciation allowance isn't affected by the timing of the asset's placed-in-service date. It is available no matter when qualifying business property is placed in service during the year.

The special deduction is available for most nonrealty business property with a 20-year or shorter useful life that qualifies for accelerated depreciation. This includes computer software and certain commercial leasehold improvements. To qualify for 50 percent bonus depreciation, the property generally must be placed in service before 2005. (A 30 percent extra depreciation allowance is available for purchases of business equipment before May 6, 2003.) Purchases of used property are not eligible for the special depreciation allowance. As shown below, the special depreciation allowance produces a large up-front tax benefit.

Illustration

If you put $100,000 of business equipment into service during 2004, the usual depreciation deduction is $20,000 (20 percent of $100,000). With the new special depreciation allowance, however, the first-year deduction increases to $60,000. That is 50 percent of $100,000, plus the usual 20 percent of the remaining $50,000 of the cost.

Illustration

For property that's subject to the stricter mid-quarter rule where relatively too much property is placed in service in the final quarter of the year, the usual deduction would be only $5,000 for fourth-quarter purchases. With the special depreciation allowance, however, the deduction would be $52,500 (50 percent of $100,000, plus 5 percent of the remaining $50,000 of the cost).

Increased Expensing

The 2003 Tax Act also increased the maximum annual dollar amount that may be expensed—that is, deducted in full rather than having to be depreciated over a number of years—from $25,000 to $100,000 for property placed in service in tax years beginning in 2003. For

2004, and 2005, the limit is increased for inflation ($102,000 in 2004 and $105,000 in 2005). The previous $200,000 threshold for phase-out of the expensing allowance was increased to $400,000 of expensing-eligible property. The limit is indexed for inflation in 2004 and 2005 ($410,000 in 2004 and $420,000 in 2005).

Off-the-shelf computer software placed in service in a tax year beginning in 2003, 2004, or 2005 now qualifies for expensing. The Act permits businesses to revoke the expensing election on amended returns without IRS consent. This may enable businesses to retroactively move expensing deductions among tax years for the maximum benefit.

The combination of the expensing allowance, bonus depreciation, and regular depreciation can enable a small business to deduct all or a significant majority of the cost of new property additions in the year of acquisition. For example, if a business acquires new property (with a five-year depreciation life) costing $300,000, it would be entitled to take a combined first-year deduction in 2004 of $220,800. The Section 179 expensing allowance will permit $102,000 to be deducted. The remaining $198,000 of acquisition cost can qualify for first-year 50 percent bonus depreciation of $99,000. Finally, the remaining $99,000 of acquisition cost can qualify for a first-year MACRS depreciation deduction of $19,800.

While tax considerations aren't paramount in a business' decision to purchase equipment, they are a factor and are more important this year because of the extra available deduction. Keep in mind that there is no AMT adjustment caused by the special depreciation allowance. As a result, the tax break won't be lost if the taxpayer is subject to the AMT.

Bigger Tax Advantages for Business Automobiles

Deductions for business automobiles are usually quite limited. The first-year deduction generally can't exceed $2,960. But to allow the

special depreciation allowance to apply for new business auto purchases, this limit temporarily has been increased to $10,610. To get
this break, an automobile must be used more than 50 percent of the
time for business. Even better, the entire purchase price of vehicles
weighing over 6,000 pounds that are used 100 percent for business
purposes can be deducted in the year of acquisition using the Section
179 expensing election discussed earlier. As with other equipment,
the added tax break isn't going to cause a business to run out and
purchase vehicles that it doesn't need. But if a business is considering
such a purchase, the extra tax break would weigh in its favor.

Retirement Plans

If this is the year that a business has decided to start a qualified retirement plan, the plan must be formally established by year-end for
contributions to be deductible this year. Contributions (up to the
limits spelled out in Chapter 3) will be deductible this year if made
by the extended tax return due date.

Businesses that miss the year-end deadline can still establish and
make deductible contributions to a simplified employee pension
plan (SEP) by their extended tax return due date. However, SEPs
have stricter coverage requirements than regular qualified plans and
generally aren't as flexible or customizable. Unlike qualified corporate retirement plans and Keogh plans, SEPs can't be set up as defined benefit pension plans, so they are less suitable for quickly
funding a large benefit for an older owner/employee.

> *Caution*
> Those who plan to set up retirement plans should immediately
> consult a retirement planning specialist. It takes time to take
> care of all of the required formalities.

Bonuses and Deferred Compensation

A corporation using accrual, rather than cash, accounting can take a current deduction for bonuses it declares this year, and that are paid within the first 2½ months of the following year. The company gets an accelerated deduction and the employee-recipient gets to defer the income. Note, however, that this planning opportunity isn't available for bonuses paid to majority shareholders or to owners with any interest in an S corporation or a personal service corporation. Compensation that is deferred for more than 2½ months is subject to different rules. In that case, the corporation's deduction is delayed until the compensation is paid to the employee. Year-end also is a good time to consider whether to establish a deferred compensation plan for key employees.

Income Deferral or Acceleration

Generally a C corporation, like an individual, will want to defer income and accelerate deductions, where possible, to reduce current taxes and defer tax liabilities into the following year. For corporations on the accrual method of accounting, this may not be as easy to do as it is for cash method individuals or businesses. However, even for them, certain recurring items may be currently deducted despite the fact that they won't be paid until the following year. There may be times also when a company can come out ahead by reversing the standard strategy and accelerating income into the current year. That's the case, for example, where the corporation is in a lower tax bracket in the earlier year than it expects to be in for the following year.

Although corporate tax rates are graduated, they don't increase in proportion to corporate taxable income. Instead, the first $50,000 is taxed at 15 percent; then the next $25,000 is taxed at 25 percent, and the $25,000 after that is taxed at 34 percent. Corporate taxable income between $100,000 and $335,000 is taxed at 39 percent, to take back the benefit of the 15 percent and the 25 percent tax brackets. Then, between $335,000 and $10 million, the marginal rate drops back to 34 percent. The effect of this is that corporations with taxable income between $335,000 and $10 million are taxed at a flat rate of 34 percent. Then, between $10 million and $15 million, the rate goes up to 35 percent, and then there's another bubble rate of 38 percent between $15 million and $18.33 million to recover the benefit of the 34 percent rate. Corporations with taxable income above $18.33 million are taxed at a flat 35 percent rate.

Legislative Alert

Congress is considering lowering the top corporate tax rate from 35 percent to 32 percent.

While all of this seems rather complex, it does present year-end tax saving strategies for corporations in some situations—especially those that are below either the 39 percent or the 38 percent bubbles this year that expect earnings to pick up next year and push them into a higher bracket. If possible, these companies should try to accelerate enough income or defer enough deductions to take advantage of the lower bracket this year.

AMT Planning

Smaller corporations are generally exempt from the AMT if their average annual gross receipts for the prior three-year period is $7.5 million or less. (New corporations are exempt for their first year, but can't average more than $5 million of annual gross receipts for the first three-year period to avoid AMT after that year.) The AMT is a complicated tax that requires many items to be refigured in a way that often reduces the tax benefit from deductions. If a company's average annual gross receipts for the current three-year period are approaching the $7.5 million mark, it should consider the impact of becoming subject to the AMT. If the current increased gross receipts is an aberration, the company probably would be better off avoiding

AMT liability if possible. If the company is growing rapidly and expects to be subject to AMT in the future, it still may benefit the company to hold off for another year before crossing the threshold.

> ### Legislative Alert
> Congress is considering increasing the small corporation exemption to relieve more small corporations from AMT liability.

Personal Holding Company Tax

To prevent high-bracket individuals from using closely held C corporations to shelter investment income and avoid the shareholder-level tax on dividend income, these corporations used to be liable for a tax at the top individual rate (38.6 percent for 2002) on their undistributed personal holding company (PHC) income. To be subject to this PHC tax, more than half of a corporation's stock had to be held by five or fewer individuals, and 60 percent of its income must come from items such as rent, royalties, interest, and dividends.

In the past, corporations near the PHC threshold of 60 percent were advised to try to avoid additional PHC income or to increase non-PHC business income to keep the PHC income percentage below 60 percent.

The 2003 Tax Act, however, has reduced the PHC tax rate to 15 percent—the same rate that now applies to dividend income. Corporations potentially subject to the personal holding company tax may consider eliminating the problem while the tax rate on dividends is only 15 percent.

Succession Planning

In addition to income tax planning, year-end is a good time for business owners to contemplate the eventual transfer of their business, whether to family members, other shareholders, key employees, or to an external third party. Owners must also take into account the financial strength of the business, financial position of the buyer, available sources of funding, collateral and financial guarantees, tax consequences to both parties, and cash flow issues. The timing of the transfer and who will retain ownership control are also critical considerations. To manage these complex issues, owners should have access to advisors who can help them make effective and timely decisions. Early planning and a sound grasp of objectives are particularly important in family owned organizations where agreement about family roles contributes to a smooth transition. There are many things to consider.

Buy-Sell Agreements

There are two distinct categories of buy-sell agreements: redemption agreements and cross-purchases. Occasionally, there will be a hybrid of the two types. Under a redemption agreement, the company will fund the buyout using its cash or debt. In a cross-purchase, the shareholder sells stock to other shareholders, not the company. This gives the buying shareholder an increase in the tax basis of his or her stock equal to the purchase price and reduces tax in the future when the stock is subsequently sold. In many cases, there is not enough cash either at the entity level or held by other shareholders to fund the entire purchase. Often, life insurance that is held individually or by a partnership is used to fund the cross-purchase portion of a buyout, with the balance funded by the company through a redemption.

Deferred Compensation

This method refers to income that is deferred until a future point in time. Typically, an employee/shareholder has been under-compensated and a deferred compensation obligation has been established to recognize that fact. Paying a retiring owner deferred compensation is advantageous to the buyer because the deferred compensation payments are tax deductible, whereas payments for his or her stock are not. However, the seller usually will prefer payment for stock, the gains from which are subject only to favorable capital gains tax rates.

Covenant Not to Compete

This is a legal contract that prohibits (for a specific period of time) a seller from competing with the buyer on the business being acquired from the seller. A buyer will frequently offer a portion of the purchase consideration in exchange for the seller signing such a restrictive covenant. This form of consideration is usually deductible to the buyer over a 15-year period, but is taxed as ordinary income for the seller.

Earn-Out (Contingent Sale Price)

This element of an acquisition refers to a transaction in which the price paid is not fixed but, instead, fluctuates based on the future performance of the acquired entity. Typically, the actual price will be tied to revenue growth or future profitability over one to five years.

The Importance of Early Planning

Often, people find it difficult to discuss issues relating to illness, retirement, or death. Business owners who avoid addressing these eventualities, however, may make succession planning a low priority, putting family members or other loved ones at financial risk. Lack of time is another often-cited factor. As in estate planning, busy owners can easily put off succession planning to some undefined future time. However, the importance of early planning cannot be overstated since it helps owners meet their stated objectives and facilitate the continuity of their businesses, to the benefit of the owners, employees, customers, and vendors.

From a financial perspective, it is often beneficial to transfer an operation on the brink of value explosion, and some owners attempt to time their transitions accordingly. Although at this stage, the business owner may have no clear picture of future control and management, this should not deter the saving of estate tax. The practical truth is that there will never be a clear picture of future control and management. The effective succession plan has considerable flexibility to deal with changing circumstances and usually involves several different types of trusts to maintain some degree of control. The important thing is not to structure the perfect plan up front, but to plan as early in the game as possible.

Don't Wait to Plan!

- Planning in advance promotes reduced estate taxes.
- Planning in advance promotes increased value for the next generation.
- In family perpetuation, owners often have an increased ability to complete long-term transfer time lines.
- Succession plans with longer time lines are inherently more flexible and may have better financial outcomes.
- Conflicting aspirations within a family regarding the timing of the transition may be addressed.

C Corporation versus S Corporation Comparison

With dividends and long-term capital gains now taxed at 15 percent under the 2003 Tax Act, the decision to conduct business as a C corporation or an S corporation should be reevaluated. In many cases, the 2003 Tax Act will make it more attractive to elect to be an S corporation by practically eliminating the prior C corporation federal tax rate advantage on ordinary income. In addition, S corporations now provide a substantial tax rate advantage for both long-term capital gains and dividends since they can pass through capital gains and dividends to shareholders undiminished by entity-level taxation. Ultimately, the conclusion will be dependent on one or more of the following factors:

- **The combined federal and state income tax rates that will be applied to income.** Movement of the federal tax rates should cause businesses to reevaluate their choice of business entity, and alternative minimum tax and state income taxes need to be factored into the analysis.

- **Whether income will be currently distributed.** If the business owners desire significant distributions of income, S corporations still have the advantage of avoiding double taxation of the income; however, the 15 percent tax rate on dividends has reduced this advantage.

- **Losses from an S corporation can flow through to the shareholders.** This remains a significant advantage of S corporations over C corporations for businesses experiencing losses.

- **The many shareholder ownership restrictions imposed on S corporations (e.g., shareholder limitations, one class of stock).** While S corporations may have tax advantages over C corporations, many businesses are unable to qualify for S corporation status. Serious consideration should be given to restructuring to qualify for S corporation status (i.e., redeem shares, eliminate multiple classes of stock).

- **The amount of LIFO recapture upon conversion to S status.** With the relatively low inflation rates recently recapturing the LIFO reserve upon conversion to S status may not be a significant cost at present.

- **Whether the business is expected to be sold before the death of the major shareholders.** Generally, buyers prefer to buy business assets as opposed to the stock of an ongoing business. By operating as an S corporation, the business owners can sell the business assets and distribute the sale proceeds with only one level of tax. The owners of a C corporation will generally pay two levels (a corporate tax on the asset sale and a shareholder tax—now reduced to 15 percent—on the distributed sale proceeds) of tax.

- **Whether the tax on built-in gains is likely to apply.** When a C corporation converts to S corporation status, the S corporation is subject to a corporate level tax on any assets sold during its first 10 years as an S corporation. This tax is imposed on the amount of gain that is present in the asset eventually sold as of the first day as an S corporation.

S corporations with C corporation earnings and profits generally will have the ability under the current tax law to purge themselves of the C corporation earnings and profits at a 15 percent tax cost to the shareholders. This may enable the S corporation to avoid the tax on excess passive income and avoid inadvertent termination of the S election from excess passive income in three consecutive tax years. This strategy may be appropriate in 2008, right before the reduced tax rates are set to expire under the sunset provision of the tax law.

C corporations with large amounts of dividend and long-term capital gain income will have a significant reason to try to convert to S corporation status if possible. The tax rate differential on this income is considerable (35 percent for C corporations versus 15 percent for S corporations).

Chapter 13 moves away from planning suggestions and techniques. It takes a close-up view of the book's basic concepts. Understanding these commonly used words and phrases is critical to making the best use of the tax planning strategies and tools discussed in this book.

A NUTS-AND-BOLTS REVIEW

Chapter 13

BASIC TAX CONCEPTS

Tax planning is a difficult, time-consuming activity at best. Fortunately, any taxpayer who reads this book is likely to have learned a great deal about effective tax planning. This chapter contains definitions of key tax terms. These definitions, which are really a combination of glossary, encyclopedia, and FAQs, constitute an indispensable reference source for taxpayers.

Earlier chapters described things you may be able to do at the end of the year to reduce your tax bill. At the end of this chapter you will find valuable suggestions for steps you can take in January as part of your tax minimization program.

Gross Income

Gross income includes all types of taxable income: wages and bonuses, taxable interest, dividends, state tax refunds, alimony, business income, capital gains, traditional IRA distributions, taxable pensions and annuities, rent, partnership distributions, unemployment compensation, and taxable Social Security benefits.

Adjusted Gross Income

Adjusted gross income (AGI) is your gross income less certain "above the line" deductions. These deductions include:

- Deductible IRA contributions (see Chapter 3).
- Health savings account contributions.
- Unreimbursed employment-related moving expenses (see Chapter 9).
- One-half of self-employment tax.
- 100 percent of health insurance premiums paid by self-employed individuals (see Chapter 9).
- Keogh and SEP contributions for self-employed individuals (see Chapter 3).
- Penalties on early withdrawals of savings.
- Student loan interest.
- Tuition and fees deduction.
- Alimony paid.
- Deduction for buying hybrid vehicles.

Your AGI affects the extent to which you can deduct medical expenses, casualty and theft losses, charitable contributions, and other miscellaneous items. At higher levels of AGI, your ability to benefit from some additional itemized deductions and personal exemptions may be reduced or eliminated (starting in 2006, this phase-out is reduced).

Modified Adjusted Gross Income

A number of tax breaks are reduced or eliminated as modified adjusted gross income (MAGI) exceeds certain levels. These include the adoption credit, the exclusion for employer-provided adoption assistance, the exclusion for interest on savings bonds used for higher education, IRA deductions, Coverdell ESAs, Roth IRAs, higher education tax credits, the child credit, and the student-loan interest deduction.

MAGI is generally higher than adjusted gross income. That's because various tax breaks that normally reduce AGI are disallowed in calculating MAGI under the different definitions.

A Tax Credit or a Deduction

Tax credits are more valuable than tax deductions because they lower your tax liability dollar for dollar. A $100 tax credit reduces your taxes by a full $100. Examples of tax credits are the HOPE scholarship and lifetime learning tax credits, the child credit, the childcare and dependent care credits, the adoption credit, and the foreign-tax credit.

A tax deduction reduces your taxes by the amount of your expenses multiplied by your marginal tax rate. The lower your tax rate, the smaller your tax benefit from a deduction. In the 35 percent tax bracket, a $100 tax deduction lowers your taxes by $35. In the 15 percent bracket, that same $100 deduction reduces your taxes by only $15.

Observation

It is unwise to pursue tax deductions by spending money on deductible items merely to cut your tax bill. You have to spend more money than you will save in taxes. Keep in mind that a tax deduction is of real value only if it reduces the after-tax cost of an expenditure that you would be inclined to make even if it were not deductible.

Taxable Income

Taxable income is the amount of income on which you actually pay tax. It is calculated by adding your income from all sources and subtracting allowable deductions and exemptions:

Taxable Income Computation

Income

Wages	$350,000
Interest, dividends, and capital gains	26,000
Business income and rental real estate income	5,000
Other income	4,500
Total income	$385,500

Adjustments to Income

Moving expenses	(3,500)
Alimony	(60,000)
Total adjustments to income	$ (63,500)
Adjusted gross income	$322,000
Itemized deductions (after phase-out applied)	(6,200)
Exemption (phased out due to income level)	None
Taxable income	$315,800

Marital Status

Your marital status on the last day of the year determines which of the four tax rate schedules applies. If you are single for most of the year, but marry on December 31, the tax law treats you as married for the entire year.

Changes in marital status can affect year-end planning. Two individuals with substantial incomes who plan to get married in 2005 might benefit from accelerating income into 2004 to avoid the so-called marriage penalty, which has been reduced, but not eliminated (see page 9).

Widows and widowers are allowed to file a joint return with their deceased spouse in the year of the spouse's death and to use joint return rates for up to two additional years if they have a qualifying dependent. Widows or widowers who may be eligible to use the more favorable married filing jointly rates in 2004, but not in 2005, could benefit from accelerating income into the earlier year (see Table 13.1).

Table 13.1			*2004 Tax Rates and Projected 2005 Tax Rates*			
Taxable Income ($)	2004 Tax ($)	Marginal Tax (%)	Taxable Income ($)	2005 Tax ($)	Marginal Tax (%)	Effective Tax Rate (%)
Single Individuals						
0	0	10	0	0	10	0
7,150	715	15	7,300	730	15	10.0
29,050	4,000	25	29,700	4,090	25	13.8
70,350	14,325	28	71,950	14,653	28	20.4
146,750	35,717	33	150,150	36,549	33	24.3
Over 319,100	92,593	35	Over 326,450	94,728	35	29.0
Married Filing Jointly						
0	0	10	0	0	10	0
14,300	1,430	15	14,600	1,460	15	10.0
58,100	8,000	25	59,400	8,180	25	13.8
117,250	22,788	28	119,950	23,318	28	19.4
178,650	39,980	33	182,800	40,916	33	22.4
Over 319,100	86,325	35	Over 326,450	88,321	35	27.1

Marginal and Effective Tax Rates

Marginal tax is the tax on the next dollar. Effective tax is the average tax rate on all of your income. For example, assume that you are married, filing a joint return, and receive:

Taxable Income	$300,000
Bonus	$ 50,000
Total Taxable Income	$350,000

The bonus is taxed at 35 percent. You would pay $17,500 ($50,000 × 35 percent) in taxes on that bonus. Your marginal tax rate is 35 percent.

Your marginal tax rate also determines the tax benefit of a deductible expense. For example, if you were in the 28 percent bracket and had $5,000 of medical expenses in excess of 7.5 percent of your AGI, which you claimed as an itemized deduction, you would reduce your taxable income by $5,000, saving $1,400 in tax dollars ($5,000 × 28 percent).

Caution

Your marginal tax rate might be less determinative of the tax benefit of a deductible expense if your income is above $145,950 for 2005, since at that income level you begin losing some of the benefit of your itemized deductions.

Your effective tax rate is the average rate at which all of your income is taxed. To determine this rate, divide your tax liability by your taxable income. If your 2004 taxable income on a joint return is $150,000 and the amount of tax due is $31,957.50, your marginal rate is 28 percent, but your effective tax rate is only 21.3 percent ($31,957.50/$150,000 = 0.213).

Your marginal tax rate can be higher than the 35 percent statutory rate due to the itemized deduction and personal exemption phase out (see page 8). The following charts show 2004 deductions and exemptions and 2005 projected thresholds:

2004 ITEMIZED DEDUCTION AND PERSONAL EXEMPTIONS

	Single	Married Joint	Separate	Head of Household
Standard Deductions				
Regular standard deduction	$4,850	$9,700	$4,850	$7,150
Additional standard deduction (elderly and/or blind taxpayers)	$1,200	$950	$950	$1,200
Kiddie tax deduction	$800	$800	$800	$800
Itemized Deduction Phase-Out				
Deductions reduced for AGI exceeding	$142,700	$142,700	$71,750	$142,700
Personal Exemption				
Each person	$3,100	$3,100	$3,100	$3,100
Personal Exemption Phase-Out				
Exemptions reduced for AGI exceeding	$142,700	$214,050	$107,025	$178,350

2005 ITEMIZED DEDUCTION AND PERSONAL EXEMPTIONS (PROJECTED)

	Single	Married Joint	Separate	Head of Household
Standard Deductions				
Regular standard deduction	$5,000	$10,000	$5,000	$7,300
Additional standard deduction (elderly and/or blind taxpayers)	$1,250	$1,000	$1,000	$1,250
Kiddie tax deduction	$800	$800	$800	$800
Itemized Deduction Phase-Out				
Deductions reduced for AGI exceeding	$145,950	$145,950	$72,975	$145,950
Personal Exemption				
Each person	$3,200	$3,200	$3,200	$3,200
Personal Exemption Phase-Out				
Exemptions reduced for AGI exceeding	$145,950	$218,950	$109,475	$182,450

The existing rules reducing itemized deductions allow you to claim at least 20 percent of your deductions regardless of your income level. This limit does not affect deductions for medical expenses, casualty losses, and investment interest.

Observation

The limit on itemized deductions increases the top marginal tax rate for high-income individuals by 1.05 percent. The phase-out of personal exemptions increases the top marginal tax rate for these families and individuals by approximately 0.75 percent for income in the phase-out range for each exemption claimed.

Observation

The 2001 Tax Act will start to eliminate the phase-outs of itemized deductions and personal exemptions beginning in 2006.

Social Security Taxes

If you are employed, you are subject to a 7.65 percent tax rate (6.2 percent for Social Security and 1.45 percent for Medicare). Your employer also pays the same rates to the government. If you are self-employed, you pay a 15.3 percent self-employment tax (12.4 percent for Social Security and 2.9 percent for Medicare). Self-employed individuals are entitled to deduct one-half of their self-employment tax. The maximum annual earnings subject to the Social Security tax are $87,900 in 2004. This amount will increase for 2005. All earnings are subject to the Medicare portion of the tax.

If you work while collecting Social Security benefits and are between age 62 and your full retirement age (e.g., 65 years and 4 months for those born in 1939), your benefits are reduced by $1 for every $2 that you earn above $11,640 in 2004 ($970 per month). This limit will increase annually. In the year you reach your full retirement age, you lose $1 for every $3 of earnings above $31,080 ($2,590 per month) in 2004, but only for those months before your full retirement age. Once you have attained your full retirement age, earnings do not cause a reduction in your benefits.

If you work while collecting benefits, you also should consider that your earnings will be subject to income tax and payroll taxes, and these earnings also may subject some of your Social Security benefits to income tax. If your AGI, plus half of your Social Security benefits, plus your tax-exempt interest equals more than $25,000 if you're single, or $32,000 if married, half of the excess amount up to half of your benefits are taxable. If your specially figured income exceeds $34,000 if single, or $44,000 if married, up to 85 percent of your Social Security Benefits may be subject to income tax.

Marriage Penalty

The marriage penalty results because the marginal tax rate is higher for married couples than it is for two single individuals with the same total income. Let's see how a married couple fared under the old rules. Assume that two single persons, each with taxable income of $100,000 in 2005, are each taxed at the 28 percent marginal rate. If these two people were married, $17,200 of their total taxable income in 2005 (the amount above $182,800) would be taxed at the 33 percent rate. Total tax for the two singles: $45,014. As a married couple, the tax would jump to $46,592, resulting in a penalty of $1,578.

If, however, one spouse has a much higher income than the other, there may be a marriage bonus. For example, a single person with $200,000 of taxable income in 2005 will pay tax at the 33 percent marginal rate on $49,850 of it. If that same person was married and his or her spouse had no income, the couple would be subject to a marginal rate of 33 percent on only $17,200 of the income using joint-return rates.

The marriage penalty has been eased somewhat by increasing the size of the 15 percent tax bracket for married taxpayers to double that of singles, and by increasing the size of the standard deduction for married taxpayers to double that of singles (see page 9 for details). Despite this, the marriage penalty still can be quite substantial for couples in the higher tax brackets.

Some married couples may benefit by filing separately. For example, it may make sense to file separately if one spouse is in a lower tax bracket and has large medical bills. The AGI threshold limiting the deduction of these medical expenses would be lower, allowing a larger deduction.

Observation

It is important to work out the numbers before deciding what to do. Over the years, Congress has added "penalty" provisions to the Tax Code to discourage married people from filing separate returns. Although filing separately may seem like a good idea for one reason or another, it might result in higher taxes overall than if you file jointly.

Accountable Plan

Business expenses reimbursed by your employer may be included as income on your Form W-2 unless your employer reimburses under an accountable plan. An accountable plan requires documentation before a return is filed of all advanced or reimbursed expenses and the return of any excess amounts. Expenses reimbursed under a nonaccountable plan can be included in your income and are deductible, as are unreimbursed employee business expenses. These are included in the miscellaneous itemized deductions category, if you have receipts and other required substantiation.

> **Observation**
>
> A nonaccountable plan is not as good as it may at first sound because miscellaneous itemized deductions can be claimed only to the extent that they total more than 2 percent of your AGI. So if your AGI is $100,000, your first $2,000 of miscellaneous expenses are not deductible. In addition, you would receive no tax benefits from the deduction of unreimbursed business expenses if you are subject to the alternative minimum tax (AMT). The AMT is described in detail in Chapter 11.

Tax Effects of Alimony

Alimony is included in the gross income of the person receiving it and is deductible by the person paying it.

> **Observation**
>
> Alimony is deducted "above the line" in arriving at AGI. Therefore, it can be claimed whether you itemize your deductions or take the standard deduction.

Payments to an ex-spouse are not treated as alimony for tax purposes if the spouses are still in the same household. It is also important to note that large decreases in the amount of alimony in the second and third years following a divorce trigger IRS concern that property settlement amounts, which are nondeductible, are being treated as alimony. There are guidelines on what payments under a divorce or separation agreement qualify as alimony for tax purposes.

For example, making rent or mortgage payments for a spouse or ex-spouse may be deductible alimony, but the value of rent-free accommodations (for example, allowing a spouse or former spouse to live without paying rent in a house you own) is not deductible.

Social Security Taxes for Domestic Employees

You must pay and withhold Social Security tax for domestic employees earning more than $1,400 during 2004. This figure will be increased for future inflation. You may report this tax liability each year as a balance due on your Form 1040, Schedule H. Be sure to increase your wage withholding or make quarterly estimated payments to pay the tax associated with these employees and avoid an estimated tax underpayment penalty.

Estimated Tax Payments

The government requires estimated payments because it prefers receiving tax payments throughout the year. Individuals with a $1,000 or greater balance due on their tax returns may be subject to an estimated tax underpayment penalty, unless certain standards are met. An interest-based underpayment of estimated tax penalty is charged if no exception applies.

In general, there are three methods that can be used to avoid an underpayment penalty:

1. Estimated tax payments and/or withholding are equal to at least 100 percent of last year's tax liability. However, if your AGI for the preceding year exceeded $150,000, your current year's estimated taxes must be 110 percent of your preceding year's tax liability to fall within this safe harbor.

2. 90 percent of your current-year tax liability is paid through estimated tax payments and/or withholding.

3. 90 percent of annualized income (determined each quarter based on actual income) is paid through estimated tax payments and/or withholding. These methods are applied to each

quarter using one-fourth of the amounts shown earlier. A different method can be applied each quarter.

Observation

The annualization method is generally best if a large part of your income is received in the latter part of the year.

Dates on Which You Must Pay Your Estimated Taxes

April 15:	Based on actual income through March 31.
June 15:	Based on actual income through May 31.
September 15:	Based on actual income through August 31.
January 15:	Based on actual income through December 31.

Caution

If you use the "90 percent of current year's tax liability" method to calculate your estimated tax payments and recognize a large gain at year-end, you could be saddled with estimated tax penalties from a shortfall in earlier payments. If you have a choice as to when you recognize the gain, remember to consider estimated taxes.

Observation

If you fall behind in estimated tax installments at the beginning of a year, you may avoid or reduce an estimated tax penalty by having additional tax withheld from your wages during the latter part of the year. Wage withholding is treated as occurring evenly over the course of the year, so one-quarter of each dollar withheld is treated as having been withheld in each quarter of the year.

You can make additional payments at any time during the year to reduce or, in some cases, eliminate potential estimated tax under-payments.

Be careful not to overpay, though, because the excess payment is essentially an interest-free loan to the government.

Observation

Use of either the annualization method or the 90 percent of cur-rent year's tax liability method is a good idea if your year-over-year income decreases or increases from one year to the next by only a small amount. But if you have a sizable increase in in-come (for instance, if 100 percent [or 110 percent for those with an AGI over $150,000] of your prior year's tax will be less than 90 percent of the tax due on your current year's income), using the "percentage of the prior year's tax liability" method al-lows the payment of lower estimated tax. This method is also far simpler, because you are using actual numbers, not estimates.

Conclusion

Rumor has it that although some people love tax planning, most people would prefer to do almost anything else. But what most of us consider a burden needn't be a nightmare or a mystery. People can understand their tax options and intelligently choose those options best suited to their needs. This book is intended to be a liberating guide, grounded in our belief that every tax problem has a solution if accurate and accessible information is available.

We have given you much to think about. Chapter 1 lays out the re-cent tax changes. The rest of the book provides a wide range of information and strategies and covers diverse areas, such as invest-ments, retirement planning, home ownership, education savings, estate planning, and year-end tax planning. It also explains many basic tax concepts. The tax laws are incredibly complex. The Internal Revenue Code, along with its regulations and related cases, procedures, and rulings, can fill whole library rooms. As difficult as the law is, specific financial, family, and business situations can complicate things further, making tax planning a highly personal and individualized undertaking.

This book offers you a foundation—information and strategies that will make most individuals aware of ideas that may work for them and help them avoid costly tax mistakes. You should supplement this new foundation in taxes by considering how your personal situation plays into tax decisions. Tax planning never occurs in a vacuum, but is just a part, albeit an important part, of an overall financial planning process.

The tax strategies described in this book have been developed from the combined experience of many PricewaterhouseCoopers professionals. However, because every individual has unique circumstances, it is important that you consult a tax professional before implementing any tax strategy described in this book or elsewhere.

January Tax Strategy Idea Checklist

Most tax help books present year-end planning ideas. We have decided to go one step further and suggest strategies that make sense to implement as early in the year as possible. Early adoption of the ideas presented in the list that follows may make sense to maximize your opportunities to defer tax, generate income that is tax-free, and/or shift assets or income out of your estate:

☑   Contribute to an IRA (see page 86).

☑   Contribute to a Coverdell Education Savings Account (see page 132).

☑   Contribute to a Section 529 plan to the amount of the state tax deduction (if available, see page 126).

☑ Make a contribution to your Keogh plan (see page 85).

☑ Consider a Roth IRA conversion (see page 91).

☑ Think about making additional gifts if you have not fully used your $1 million gift tax exemption (see page 161).

☑ Make payments that were due in 2004 that you deferred to 2005 because of the AMT (see page 227).

☑ Purchase the annual maximum of Series I bonds (see page 213).

☑ Make $11,000 ($22,000 for married couples) annual exclusion gifts (see page 163).

☑ Exercise Incentive Stock Options, so that you have a full year to decide whether to sell the stock and be taxed as a non-qualified stock option (see page 69).

ABOUT THE AUTHORS

Michael B. Kennedy is a Human Resource Services partner and national director of PricewaterhouseCoopers Personal Financial Services, which provides comprehensive financial planning services to high net worth individuals, corporate executives, business owners, and entrepreneurs. Michael has been with the firm for more than 29 years. Michael is a CPA and member of the American, Pennsylvania, and New Jersey Institutes of Certified Public Accountants and holds the Personal Financial Specialist designation. He has both a BS in Economics and a MBA from Rider University. Michael is an adjunct member of the Villanova University Graduate Tax Program. He is a member of the board of trustees of Rider University and was most recently honored by his alma mater with a lifetime achievement award from the School of Business.

Bernard S. Kent is a Human Resource Services partner in PricewaterhouseCoopers Personal Financial Services practice. He has more than 30 years of experience encompassing all phases of tax planning and personal financial counseling. He is frequently quoted in numerous national periodicals, including the *Wall Street Journal, New York Times, Forbes, Fortune, U.S. News and World Report,*

Investor's Business Daily, BusinessWeek, Barron's, Kiplinger's, and *Inc.,* and was chosen three times by *Worth* magazine as one of the best financial advisors in the country. He is the past chairman of the personal financial planning committee of the Michigan Association of Certified Public Accountants. Bernie received his BA in Economics from Oakland University and his JD from the University of Michigan Law School.

INDEX